Beyond Consequences, Logic, and Control

A Love Based Approach to Helping Children With Severe Behaviors

Beyond Consequences, Logic, and Control

A Love Based Approach to Helping Children With Severe Behaviors

Heather T. Forbes, LCSW

Beyond Consequences Institute

Beyond Consequences, Logic, and Control

A Love Based Approach to Helping Children With Severe Behaviors

ISBN 0-9777040-3-3

First Edition 2008
Second Edition 2009

Published by:
Beyond Consequences Institute, LLC
Boulder, CO

Cover Photograph:
Lisa Zader (www.CapturedByTheLensPhotography.com)

Book Design:
Tyler Thomas

Dedication

∎

This book is dedicated to
the loving memory of my mom,

DOROTHY ALLABEN TALBERT
(1934-2008)
A woman who modeled to me
the tenacity, dedication, and fortitude
it takes to stand up for
the rights of children.

Table of Contents

■

A Note to the Reader

■

    This book will offer you a completely new understanding of how to love and parent your children. It comes from not only my research as a professional or from my experience as a family therapist. This information presented to you in the following pages comes mainly from my direct experience as a mother. Both my children exhibited severe behaviors that put my family into a state of utter chaos. As I sought help from professionals and parenting books, the madness only seemed to intensify. The physical violence my son brought into my home was beyond my comprehension for such a young child. The emotional violence I then returned to him from my own being was terrifying to me. I kept asking myself, "What has gone so terribly wrong? How have we fallen from a place of love, commitment, joy, and excitement to a place of panic, violence, resentment, and sheer hatred?"

    What was converging in my home was generations of untouched trauma, a backlog of pain that was never addressed directly, most of which was mine to own. Yet, the more than 200 parenting books that I had purchased off of the Internet night after night never mentioned this. These parenting books focused on how to get my children to behave. They listed in detail how to create a point chart in order to make my children be accountable for their behaviors. These books presented their information in a way that urged me to take control and, in fact, demand control and respect from my children. The common thread running through all these parenting books was that children needed to be shaped into respectful little beings. They were the clay and I was to mold them. As the parent, I needed to stay above the emotional quagmire that was overwhelming my children in order to stay in charge and to be the strong figure directing their lives.

    What these parenting books did not address was me. I have come to realize that my state of mind and my state of heart is the key influence in how my family operates. It is not about techniques because love is not a technique. It is not about loving my children through controlling measures. It is not about right or wrong or judgment to be handed down in order to create moral and ethical children. It is not about "daring to discipline." It is quite the opposite. It is about daring to love and parent without relying on external measures of control, authority, or consequences.

We have somehow come to believe that love is not enough. In fact, there are parenting books with titles that indicate that love is only a start[1], that love is not enough[2], or that there are limits to love and hope[3]. I challenge you as a parent to honestly look at these fearful titles and question how the greatest and most powerful force known to mankind is not enough! Love is always the answer because love never fails.

I have come to realize that the issue is not that love is not enough, it is that we as a human species do not really know what love is. We do things that we call "love" while all along they are full of fear, judgment, resentment, and control. In order to understand how to be loving parents, it will take first understanding what love is. Loving ourselves is the next step in learning to be loving parents. This concept is a simple mathematical fact. I cannot give something that I do not have. I cannot give you ten dollars if I do not have ten dollars. Thus, I cannot give my children love if I do not have love.

Yet, going back to the 200 parenting books, this concept was missed. That is exactly why I had over 200 books! The information wasn't working because these books were missing the key ingredient to connecting with my children: Me! It was like baking 200 loaves of bread and each time leaving out the yeast. Over and over again, while expecting a beautiful fluffy loaf, I was left with a flattened wad of flour and water, void of life.

It takes courage to switch to the new understanding presented in this book. Shifting your perspective to a new paradigm, a new way of living, will challenge you at your deepest core. Yet, it has the potential to be one of the greatest paradoxes you will ever experience. That which you tried to control will now be occurring naturally. The authority you have been battling to obtain is actually something you have within yourself. The motivation you have been working to instill in your children was there all along. You will see that the silence of listening is far more effective than the noise of lecturing. You will realize that showing respect in the face of disrespect, love in the face of fear, peace in the face of chaos, and trust in the face of betrayal, will teach more to your children than all the preachers in the pulpit on Sunday morning combined.

■

The silence of listening is far more effective than the noise of lecturing.

■

The challenge may be that it appears too simple to be effective. The paradox is that we have come to believe that for something to be effective, it has to be complex, and if something is simple, it cannot be effective.

Yet, quite the opposite is true. Albert Einstein said, *"Any intelligent fool can make things bigger and more complex . . . it takes a touch of genius and a lot of courage to move in the opposite direction."*

While the concepts presented in this book are easy, they are hard to implement. Yet, the more you realize the true essence of love, the more you will flow with confidence in knowing that your children will find their way without the traditional measures in place, and you will come to trust that real control comes through your loving, nurturing, nonjudgmental, and predictable influence. As a *Beyond Consequences* parent, you will not always know ahead of time how to respond in each situation, yet as you stay in a loving space in every situation, the answers will emerge. That is the power of love. Never allow your fear to constrict the answers from surfacing.

Your children are gifts to you so that you no longer are stuck living as a master of fear. I invite you to read this book with an open mind and heart. It will give you the knowledge and understanding you need to become a master of love and a master at parenting your children, free of consequences, free of fear, and free of control.

Press on,
Heather T. Forbes, LCSW

P.S. I strongly encourage you to read the first volume, at least chapters one through four, to gain a foundational understanding of the *Beyond Consequences* principles. The information presented here in Volume 2 begins where the first volume ended and is an expansion and an evolution of the *Beyond Consequences* paradigm. Enjoy!

A Life-Transforming Offer!

My heart and soul has been poured into the following pages, along with years of research, experience, hurt, and joy. You have worked hard to find answers for your child, and I don't want to waste your time or money. For the time you take to study this book thoroughly and put the ideas into place, I'd like to offer you a day of transformation ... a coupon for two to attend any one of my upcoming Beyond Consequences Live seminars – free. If you've enjoyed this book, you'll love the live seminar. To redeem the discount, just bring your copy of the book to the seminar. Sign-up online at: **www.BeyondConsequencesLive.com**

This is good for the attendance of one single parent and support person, or one couple. Valid only after the purchase of the book. Book must be shown at the seminar.

Upcoming Locations:
Los Angeles, CA
San Francisco, CA
Dallas, TX
Denver, CO
Chicago, IL
St. Louis, MO

For more information, log on to: www.BeyondConsequencesLive.com

Finally, here's my 100% guarantee to you:
If, after putting into place any of the ideas in this book for a consistent period of two weeks, you do not see at least a 50 percent reduction in your child's negative behavior, return the book to me and I will refund every penny of your money, no questions asked!

However, if what you try works, send me an e-mail letting me know what you tried, how it worked, and how long it took for you to see results. Just e-mail me at info@beyondconsequences.com. I am serious about you, your child, and your family, but most of all, I am serious when I say that love never fails!

PART ONE

The Principles of a New Understanding

CHAPTER ONE

From Research to Love

■

"The greatest science in the world,
in heaven and on earth, is love."
– Mother Teresa

I recently made a trip to a local university for a "day off" to do research. Yes, my idea of fun is research! (I'm certain there is some sort of pathology associated with such a statement.)

So I sit down at the computer, breathing in and experiencing the joy of my moment in the here and now . . . I'm ready to embark on the latest and greatest research. I locate the perfect search engine to scan all the psychological journals. Yes, the excitement is building. I place my fingers on the keyboard and salivate as I taste the success of a page of sweet results.

I type the classic acronym for the end-all-of-end-all mental health disorders for traumatized children: RAD *(reactive attachment disorder).* Within seconds I find a list of more than 3,000 articles. How much time do I have, I wonder? How many of these can I make it through before I need to leave to pick up my own children (formerly diagnosed with RAD).

I scan through the most recent articles. I print them out. Before long, I have a pile of articles more than two inches thick. As I am scanning through the abstracts, being led through percentages, dissecting the statistical data from Pearson's® to alpha scores, and weeding through the explanations of the research methodology, I come to one very important realization: these researchers have little or no experience with attachment-challenged children with severe behaviors.

Do they really know what it is like to live day in and day out with a child who continually lives in a fear state, resulting in a child who is disrespectful, disobedient, and simply beyond comprehension on his best day? Do they know what it is like to give and give and give to a child who is too stressed out to receive? Do these researchers understand what it is like to be a parent at your brink, curled up in a fetal position on the bathroom floor, just praying to make it through one more day?

The explanations of raising children with difficult behaviors are written in this research in such an objective form (which is appropriate in formal peer-reviewed journal articles), but it takes away from the reader being able to comprehend the intensity of being a parent or caretaker living in the midst of fear and trauma. Here is one such statement: "The high prevalence of RAD raises therapeutic challenges for those involved in the care of children." So, now when your friends ask, "How are you?" you can say, "Well, I'm therapeutically challenged right now!"

The majority of the articles expanded on the actual criteria of reactive attachment disorder and discussed the inherent problems in the DSM-IV (the Diagnostic and Statistical Manual of Mental Disorders – the "bible" of mental health disorders). Many articles discussed the limitations of studies and the limits of what attachment theory can tell us.

After about two hours of researching and printing copies of these articles, I found myself staring at half a tree of paper, wondering how this was going to help parents. The concluding remarks in many of the articles ended with bleak comments such as, " . . . there is little in the way of evidence-based treatment for this disorder, and those treatments which do exist are controversial."

What?! All this research, money, and time only to end with a bleak, hopeless statement like this? What about the children? What about the moms and dads struggling to create peaceful, loving homes? There appears to be a wide ravine spanning academia and "when the rubber hits the road" parenting. While both sides have the common goal of creating positive change, the connection of the two is far and wide.

So where do we go from here? I take a deep breath and calm my own nervous system. "Where do we go from here?" I ask myself again. Then I realize it is not about going somewhere, but returning somewhere.

The answer is that we need to go right back to the beginning. We simply need to get back to the basics and return to love. No statistical data is needed, no research methodologies need to be designed and, most importantly, no limitations exist with love.

In returning to love, we then have to ask, "Do we really understand the true meaning of love?" Many of us were raised in dysregulated families without the love model that we needed. We later found ourselves in relationships that defined love to equal pain, rejection, and abandonment.

Redefining our love program becomes the first order of business in implementing a

■

Then I realize it is not about going somewhere, but returning somewhere.

■

love-based parenting model. This is where my day of research shifts. Instead of my keyword being a mental health disorder like ADHD or RAD, my keyword becomes "love." What comes up is both love and unconditional love. I ask myself, "Is there a difference?" Are they not one and the same? Is this term not redundant? So I continue for a couple of hours and conclude the following to be the meaning of love:

Love is kindness, caring, and acceptance without judgment, all the time, under no conditions. Love says *"I accept you as you are."* Love says, *"I accept your behaviors at this very moment because I accept you."* Love trusts that your child has the ability to change his behaviors once he feels accepted unconditionally.

One website offered this from an unknown author:

> *"I love you as you are as you seek to find your own special way to relate to the world, or the way you feel is right for you. It is important that you are the person you want to be and not someone that I or others think you should be. I realize I cannot know what is best for you, although perhaps sometimes I think I do. I've not been where you have been, viewing life from that angle you have; I do not know what you have chosen to learn, how you have chosen to learn it, with whom or in what time period. I have not walked life looking through your eyes, so how can I know what you need?"*

Unconditional love is love without requiring anything in return – love no matter what. It is telling your child, *"I love you"* without expecting him* to say *"I love you"* in return. Love is asking your child, *"What's wrong, Billy? You seem upset."* while in return getting, *"I don't want to talk about it! I hate you!"* yet still not reacting with negativity. Love is accepting that your child is in a state of fear when he is not able to connect with you at that moment. Love responds to such dysregulation by saying, *"I'm here when you are ready, Billy."*

Love celebrates the moment of victory and lets go of the past. When your teenage daughter comes back after running away from home without telling you where she was, you say, *"I'm so glad you're home. I've really missed you. We need to celebrate your return."*

Love stays focused on the relationship and the experience, not the outcome. Love trusts that if the experience is void of fear, the outcome will take care of itself. If the child is asked to take the garbage out and he refuses to do so, the parent stops and focuses on the relationship.

The parent recognizes that there must be a disconnect between the parent and the child and moves in to repair the disconnect, recognizing that the garbage is secondary at this moment. The parent says to the child, *"You seem pretty stressed right now. Hard day at school?"*

Love begins in loving ourselves first. Self-love allows us to validate and accept ourselves without requiring others to do the same for us. A parent who loves herself understands that when her child stomps off and whispers insults under his breath that she is still a good parent. **Love recognizes that the behavior of a child does not determine the parent's effectiveness.** The parent with self-love is not looking for her child to validate her.

> ■
> *Love trusts that if the experience is void of fear, the outcome will take care of itself.*
> ■

Most importantly, love allows children to have their emotional space. When children have emotional space, free of fear, free of judgment, free of control, they then have the capacity to find their own way back to love. Love recognizes that the teaching of the life lesson is only effective when the child is regulated and back in relationship. So later that night, mom sits with her son and says, *"Today when you stomped off and whispered those words under your breath, it was disrespectful to me. I understand you were frustrated, but I know we can work this out in a nicer way between the two of us. Would you work on this with me?"*

My day of academic research shifted me right back to the place I needed to be. When we lose ourselves in an overindulgence of intellect, technology, analysis, rationalization, and complexity, we lose the primal focus of our purpose here on earth. Love really is enough. It simply takes putting unconditional love into action to help any child find his way back to this place of peace, joy, confidence, and safety. Implement love-based parenting, as described in this book, and you will find answers, and more importantly, you will find your children and lead them back to their true essential state of love.

---

* *Throughout this book, the child is referred to as masculine in order to avoid clumsy constructions (except in the chapter on self-injury, the feminine form is used as this behavior is predominately seen in girls.)*

CHAPTER TWO

Love-Based Parenting
■

"Where there is great love
there are always miracles."
– Willa Cather

What defines the term love-based? At first glance you might ask yourself, "Aren't most parenting approaches love-based? Parents love their children, so how could parenting not be of love?"

The truth is that so many of the parenting techniques we have used or that were used on us as children are actually based in fear, not love. They are fear-based techniques disguised as love. Motivating children to behave or to respond appropriately to parental requests using sticker charts, point systems, consequences, or removal of privileges is about fear, not love.

To see this perspective clearly, it first requires us to understand love and how it relates to being unconditional. We must make the distinction between conditional love and unconditional love to truly become a safe base for our children. Thus, to see more deeply into love, it requires us to experience our children more deeply.

If you are reading this book because your child does not respond well to traditional parenting techniques, I want you to celebrate; if your child responded well to traditional techniques, you would miss the opportunity to challenge everyday assumptions of effective parenting. Your child is giving you the cause to examine major institutions and accepted standards right in your own home. You are joining major historical figures in challenging these institutions – you are joining the ranks of Martin Luther King, Jr., Jane Addams, Mother Teresa, and other activists and reformers. Remember that one person can make a difference!

■

When the parent is more concerned for his needs than the needs of the child, then fear exists – fear-based parenting exists.

■

When Does Love-Based Parenting Exist?
Love-based parenting exists when the concern for the needs (emotional, physical, or relational) of the child becomes as significant to the parent as the parent's own needs. Conversely, when the

parent is more concerned for her needs than the needs of the child, then fear exists – fear-based parenting exists.

For example, if a parent finds herself in a frustrated state, demanding that the child respect her ("Look at me when I'm talking to you!") or that the child change his tone of voice ("Don't use that tone of voice with me!"), then she is, at that moment, more concerned with her own emotional wellbeing than with her child's emotional wellbeing. While we typically justify this type of interaction under the premise that the child needs to learn how to act socially appropriate, the core issue of being disconnected with the child's wellbeing goes unacknowledged.

Use this idea to gauge where you are in the moment with your child. Stay mindful of whether you are more concerned about your own wellbeing or your child's wellbeing. Genuine love puts you in a place where the two are equal. This empathetic connectedness, both to you and your child, is a requirement of love-based parenting. Maintaining this balance is always more important than the task or parental request at hand. When a parent can demonstrate this to the child, the child develops a sense of security and in return develops the ability to self-regulate in times of stress, and negative behaviors disappear.

Love-based parenting elevates the importance of the relationship to the highest position. No homework assignment, no chore, and no social etiquette is ever more important than the parent-child relationship. Maintaining connectedness and attunement, thereby sustaining the balance of love of self and love of child, is the primal outcome of every interaction the parent has with the child. When this is achieved, the other less significant items will take care of themselves. The ultimate challenge in reaching this goal is that children both want and need autonomy (independence), yet they are biologically engineered to be in relationships and to belong (dependence). This clash between the two is compounded by American culture where there is a powerful emphasis on the individual rather than on relationships, on independence rather than dependence.

> ■
> *Love-based parenting elevates the importance of the relationship to the highest position.*
> ■

As a parent, this need for both connection and separation can feel more like a crash than a clash, especially when raising children with trauma histories. This is due to the child's early history of experiencing fear and pain within the parent-child relationship. Vulnerability came at a tender age – an age where the child was designed to experience attunement, safety, attention, acceptance, validation, tolerance, patience, kindness, and joy. Instead, the child's experience was rampant with abandonment, rejection, loss, isolation, fear, and anger. The result is a child who stays in a place of self-focused survival, unable to connect yet terrified of being alone.

Our role as parents is to then teach a new definition of love (or more correctly, the true definition of unconditional love), dissolving the negative experiences of the past in order to move into the parent-child relationship safely and comfortably. We need to realize that the child cannot always return the love he is given because he is unable to move out of his self-preservation state of fear at the moment due to the painful experiences of his past.

Understanding Survival. As parents, we hold the ability to help define and re-define our child's relational experiences. The power of parenting is an amazing responsibility we carry. Parenting children who either come into our homes from negative experiences or who had unavoidable traumatic experiences within our homes puts us in a place not only to create positive relational experiences, but to overcome negative relational experiences. This is what makes this responsibility so much more difficult than "typical" parenting. And this is what makes it even more of a requirement to implement a love-based parenting model. It is an absolute necessity because we are dealing with children who are living in a place of survival.

To understand this term "survival," a quick study of the brain is necessary. The brain is a network of individual cells called neurons within the nervous system. It is an organ whose specialized function is for its linked collection of similar cells to stand ready to perform – ready for action. This grouping of cells serves a primal purpose: survival.

When trauma happens, the signals become automatic and programmed into the body's stress response system. At a primal level, there is no prize for second place. Hence, the quest for survival is intense, unbending, and relentless. A child or adult in survival answers not to the rules of logic, but to raw survival instincts.

The brain is divided up into three distinct sub-brains: the reptilian brain, the limbic

> ■
>
> *At a primal level, there is no prize for second place. A child or adult in survival answers not to the rules of logic, but to raw survival instincts.*
>
> ■

brain, and the neocortical brain (see Figure 2.1). The reptilian brain is steeped in the physiology of survival with its only goal being that of sustaining life. It houses vital life functions, neurons that control breathing, swallowing, and heart rate. (It is interesting to note that in a person who is literally "brain-dead," it is this part of the brain that is still operational.)

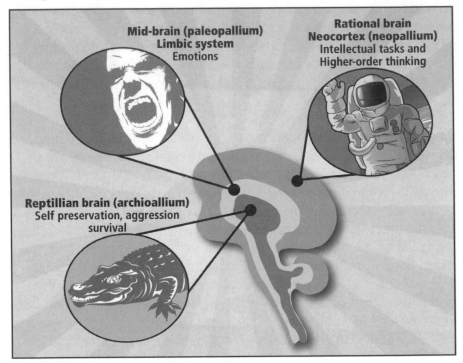

Figure 2.1

The second brain, the limbic brain, is what begins to distinguish mammals from reptiles. Your high school biology class made the distinction between reptiles and mammals from a list that included the following: (1) they grow hair instead of scales, (2) they are self-warming, and (3) they bear their young internally instead of leaving them in the external environment in eggs. Yet, in this list, one distinct difference was left out. Mammals form close-knit social groups and parents nurture and safeguard their young from the dangers of the world outside of their social groups or families. A mammal will not hesitate to risk its life to protect its young or its mate. Yet, a reptile will sit and watch the death of its young without flinching. It is the limbic brain that gives mammals the capacity to take on this life protector role and to have an intense awareness and concern for others.

The neocortex is the third brain and in humans, the largest. Speaking, writing, planning, and reasoning all originate in the neocortex. Our level of awareness and our conscious motor control, otherwise known as our "will," are found in this brain. Our ability to focus attention, to think abstractly, to problem-solve, to reason, and to plan makes its headquarters in the neocortex.

When parenting children with severe behaviors, it is critical to understand that, of these three brains, the functions of the first two are involuntary. Words, logic, consequences, and reason mean absolutely nothing to at least two of the three brains. To help a child access this third brain, it takes creating a calm, secure, safe, and loving environment, rich with relationship. It takes having positive relational experiences over and over to provide the opening for the child to move from this place of survival, out of the first two brains and into the third brain (the control center of one's will). Creating such experiences is our responsibility as parents. It is not our child's responsibility to give back in this parent-child relationship for the moment because he simply is unable to do so when he is in his reptilian brain. It is like asking a kindergartner to do calculus. Impossible.

Out of Survival – Into Relationships. We must remember that a child caught in this place of survival cannot partake of or value a parent's point of view more than his own. The road to healing comes in the parent first valuing and partaking in the child's viewpoint, no matter how illogical or irrational it may seem to the parent. For the child, it is his reality, thus it is his truth. Validating him, understanding him, and respecting him (notice agreeing with him is not listed here) will create the path to moving the child from fear to love. As the child experiences these qualities, he is learning how to do the same for others. He is experiencing a shift from survival to relationship. This type of experiential knowledge far outpowers a parent lecture on how and why he should be caring about others or why he should be doing what he was told.

We are given more years to create these positive experiences with our children than any other species, on the planet. Humans have the longest childhood compared to other

■

We must remember that a child caught in this place of survival cannot partake of or value another parent's point of view more than his own.

■

primate species and most of it is spent relying on parents and others to meet the most basic of needs. We are configured for relating to others, and to develop this ability to its fullest, we are given this time in our childhood.

Unfortunately, when this time in childhood is not used in a positive way, the impact on adulthood is significant. As the child grows up and then attempts to navigate through adult relationships within a relational framework that is either distorted or flawed, dysfunctional and failed relationships are often the result. Creating a new framework – one based in love, not fear – needs to be the most important goal for parents to get a child back on track.

Loving our children through our actions and our commitment to their wellbeing happens in every interaction we have with them. Every moment is an opportunity to help calm their first two brains, giving them the ability to access their higher-thinking brain. Every moment is a moment to create a positive experience between you and your child to develop healthy relational imprints. For you individually, every moment is a chance to challenge conventional parenting based in fear in order to develop a deeper understanding within yourself as to the nature of unconditional love.

■

Every moment is an opportunity to help calm their first two brains, giving them the ability to access their higher thinking brain.

■

CHAPTER THREE

Staying in the Present Moment

■

*"There is never a time when your life
is not 'this moment.' "*
– Eckhart Tolle

As discussed in Chapter 1, most research presents the data in a sterile and objective format. However, the good news is that there is research that is becoming much more "human" and more science that is connecting with basic life principles such as love, empathy, intuition, and mindfulness. It is not uncommon to be at a neuroscience conference and hear nationally and internationally recognized researchers standing up and giving examples of how to be present and how to liberate yourself from judgment by loving yourself. Isn't this great? This means that brain science is giving us the scientific evidence that love really is the answer.

Brain science is teaching us how important it is to be "present" in the moment to create safe, loving, and trusting relationships with first ourselves, then with our children. Dr. Daniel Siegel, author of *The Mindful Brain: Reflection and Attunement in the Cultivation of Well-Being,* defines being mindful in the moment as "being aware in the present moment, on purpose, non-judgmentally."[1]

For example, when you are in the shower, do you feel the water on your body? If you are walking through a garden, are you aware of each step and the flowers and smells around you? Becoming consciously aware at the level of all the senses is about living in the fullness of each moment. Living in the present is essential to cultivate well-being and to connect first with yourself and then with your children. To connect in relationship, you must be present in the "here and now."

When you are in the present moment, you become more fully attuned to your children. Your level of connection with them deepens. You become a safer person. This fosters a relational environment conducive to trust, love, and healing. Secure attachment cannot be created if you are living out of the past or worrying about the future. Attachment happens in the moment. Staying present with your child is the key to attachment, healing, and strong relationships.

While strong relationships are the ultimate goal with your children, it is also important to note that before this is possible, a different dynamic needs to come to fruition – and that is within you. Self-observation, to be inside your own mind, observing yourself is necessary to develop your mindfulness. It takes being aware, staying non-judgmental, and not reacting. Being in the present moment is about becoming your own best friend. Loving yourself, forgiving yourself, and accepting yourself is the pivotal point in creating a healing place within you in order for your child to find healing via his relationship with you. Healing happens through relationships, and the more you love yourself, the more your child can love himself.

■

Healing happens through relationships and the more you love yourself, the more your child can love himself.

■

Neuroscience tells us that when we have an emotional response to something, your body works to return to equilibrium. Being present is using your middle prefrontal cortex (part of the neocortex) to return to this state of equilibrium. The prefrontal cortex is the part of the brain that processes thoughts and words, and it is responsible for the "executive functions," such as working memory, decision-making, planning and judgment. This gives you the ability to literally use your words through the power of the mind to bring you back to a state of equilibrium. Yet, it is not about intellectualizing or rambling but specifically using words to connect you to yourself and to your surroundings in the present moment.

When your child is misbehaving and you become upset, your mind will work to return to equilibrium. Your previous experiences will be the automatic path your mind will take. If your programming says to yell or scream, then that is what you will do if you are not in a mindful place. Overcoming your parental responses means taking charge of your mind and installing new parenting programs (see Chapter 4 for a more extensive discussion on parenting programs).

The following are essential characteristics to being present in the moment:

1. Regulation
2. Attunement
3. Emotional Equilibrium
4. The Space to Choose
5. "Walking in Another's Shoes"
6. Linking

7. Calming the Amygdala
8. Your Gut Instinct

Regulation. The body is designed as the mechanism for keeping coordination and balance. Hormones in the bloodstream, the immune system, and the nervous system communicate with the brain and body to help regulate our systems. Early life experiences and relationships give us the ability to develop (or not develop) this system of regulation within us.

Children with trauma histories have not had enough positive life experiences to know what bodily regulation feels like. Their systems have been living in stress and have not developed the ability to regulate at the body level. Their systems live in a constant state of overdrive – a state of dysregulation. That is their normal which affords them only a small window of stress tolerance (see the following chapter for a more extensive discussion on window of tolerance). They live only minutes, if not seconds away, from their breaking point constantly. Helping your child shift from this place of dysregulation to a place of regulation becomes your primary responsibility. Parenting through the techniques described in this book sets the stage for this type of healing to be possible. Yet before any of these strategies can be implemented, it is imperative that you understand that your child's state of dysregulation is a physiological condition. This will provide you far more patience than seeing your child as making poor choices, being intentionally disobedient, or manipulating you.

One of the first changes you can make is to begin using the words "regulation" and "dysregulation" in place of "good" or "bad." If Susie is behaving "badly," that simply means Susie is "dysregulated." Her system is out of balance and she is in a state of dysregulation. These two terms allow for change because if someone is dysregulated, that implies they also have the capacity to be regulated. These are two states we move in and out of all day long.

Let's take the example of when you are sleeping in a peaceful and regulated state. BAMB! The alarm clock goes off. You become dysregulated. You turn off the alarm and shift back into a state of regulation. As you make your way out of bed, you stub your toe on the dresser. You shift back into a state of dysregulation. You catch your breath, shake your foot, and you are back to a regulated state. This continues all morning; then you get your cup of coffee. At last, regulation at its finest. Then you drive to work and realize you forgot the report you worked on until midnight and it is due to your boss in 10 minutes. Dysregulation strikes again. As an adult, you have a fairly well developed regulatory system. You can shift in and out of regulation and dysregulation without much effort because you have "emotional flexibility."

A child with difficult or severe behaviors does not have the ability to shift back and forth with ease. He needs your assistance, through your ability to stay present with him to be able to develop his ability to self-regulate. Your ability to maintain your state of regulation is paramount in this process.

Attunement. Attunement is defined as the sense that one human is sending signals to another person and these signals are being received and understood. The receiver of these signals maintains his state of regulation yet resonates with what the other person is communicating. It is like a dance between two people.

If the child senses that the parent has "tuned him out," then the child's system is not being fed the signals it needs to feel safe. The parent's role is to maintain a sense of self and to maintain a state of regulation while at the same time receiving the child's signals. For the parent receiving these signals, the key is to not let the child's signals become too overwhelming where the parent shifts and becomes dysregulated.

However, attunement between the child and parent may not always be possible in the moment. Some children may not be able to respond to the parent while in the midst of their stress and overwhelm. A child who is not listening to his parent or giving any indication that he is receiving the parent's signals is a child incapable of attunement at the moment. (This is the time to calm the stress, not yell and get angry that he is not paying attention). As this child is met with unconditional acceptance and given safety and security, he will, over time, be able to shift to a place of being able to receive the parent's signals. It takes removing the fear and adding love. Fear from a parent will only breed more fear within the child and more disconnect. Love is the answer to interrupting this fear cycle.

Emotional Equilibrium. We are designed to experience enough emotions so that life has meaning but not too much so that we are left feeling overwhelmed. When our emotional equilibrium is off, we feel out of control. Yet, it is important in early life experiences to have mild swings of arousal to feel the discomfort of the emotions to learn to regulate.

Since children with trauma histories have typically only felt extreme swings of intense emotions, they feel overwhelmed and out of control most of the time. The parent's role is to start modulating the environment to provide less external stressors in order for their internal system to find more balance. The goal is to reduce the child's swings from one emotional state to the next by providing the child a safe environment.

For parents, meditation and contemplative prayer are ways to begin to develop internal equilibrium within themselves. It is a practice that parents should consider making a part of their daily routines. Becoming familiar with yourself allows you more tolerance, love, and acceptance for yourself. This in turn will give you a greater ability to be accepting towards your child in times of stress and behavioral chaos.

The Space to Choose. Our brain's amygdala is geared for survival. It is reactive and takes immediate action when it senses danger. There is no "space" between the time we encounter a stimulus and our reaction (see Figure 3.1). While this is an excellent design to keep us alive and safe, it is an ineffective way to live our daily lives. Newton postulated that, *"Every single action has an equal and opposite reaction."* What we now need to consider is how to enlarge this space between the action and the equal and opposite reaction so we are not living our lives in a state of trigger response mode. In his book, *The 8th Habit,* Dr. Stephen Covey bases much of his work on the concept of enlarging this space. He writes, *"Between stimulus and response there is a space. In that space lies our freedom and power to choose our response. In those choices lie our growth and happiness."* [2]

Dysregulated Parent

Regulated Parent

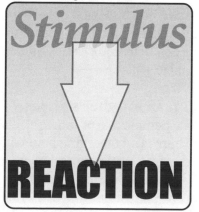

Figure 3.1

To be able to access this space, you must be out of survival and operating from your third brain, the neocortex. It is in this higher brain that you will be able to process your response with more meaning and more intent, having control over your impulsivity. If you grew up with unconditional love and support, you naturally have a large space between the stimulus and your response. However, if you are like the majority of the population, this space is very small. Learning to live in the moment and being present allows you to enlarge this space which then allows you to be able to connect with your children. It is in this space you will find healing and peace within your home.

Using consequences, logic, and control will only keep this child looping in his internal fear cycle, sectioned off from his ability to think clearly and act consciously and without the needed help to enlarge his space.

If a child has no impulse control, then his amygdala is firing without adequate communication from the third brain. With this understanding, it becomes clear this child is not making the conscious decision to grab, hit, or act impulsively. He has no space! The child needs a parent figure to help him learn how to regulate and enlarge his space between the stimulus and the response. It takes the parent living in the present moment to first accept the child where he is, understand and acknowledge the child's struggles and pain, create safety through the parent-child relationship, and to teach the child how to do it differently the next time. Using consequences, logic, and control will only keep this child looping in his internal fear cycle, sectioned off from his ability to think clearly and act consciously, without the needed help to enlarge his space.

"Walking in Another's Shoes." Empathy is the ability to put yourself in the perspective of someone else, essentially walking in another's shoes. There is an emerging field within brain science called social neuroscience. Social neuroscience focuses on how the brain functions in social interactions and studies the circuitry in two people's brains that become activated while they interact. Scientists have determined it is our "mirror" neurons that are responsible for our ability to feel what others are feeling. Mirror neurons "reflect back an action we observe in someone else, making us mimic that action or have the impulse to do so."[3] This gives us the ability to be empathetic with someone else and literally feel them at a neurological level. Studies are showing that it is indeed our default wiring to be empathetic and to attend to the needs of others.[4] What throws us off track from this natural state is stress. When we are stressed out, we are self-absorbed and we can focus only on ourselves which keeps us from being able to make use of these mirror neurons in human relationships. We lose the ability to empathize with others and with our children.

Yet, children need their parents to really "get them." They need to be understood and they need empathetic connection. Children with trauma histories typically have such difficult early experiences that they resonate at intense dysregulated levels. They need their parents to connect with them and demonstrate empathy to their pain. In doing so, it helps the child shift out of his state of survival because the parent is joining with the child and connecting with the child at a neurological level.

These types of interactions are also the best way to teach a child empathy. Findings on mirror neurons are showing that mirror neurons appear to be necessary to the way children learn. If you want to teach your child how to walk in the shoes of others, it first takes walking in the shoes of your child. You simply cannot give something you have not received.

Linking. Staying present allows us to have insight into ourselves and to have more self-awareness. It keeps us aware of who we are, where we have been, and where we are going. This affords us the ability to "link" our experiences and ultimately change and create our future. We have the ability to see into the past and say, "Hey, this is where I've been." The mind can then link it to the present, saying, "This is what I'm experiencing right now." Finally, the mind can link it to the future, saying, "This is how I'm going to respond next time." The mind has past, present, and future integration. If you do not intentionally engage in this linking process, it is like the old adage, "if you don't know the history, you're bound to repeat it." This is because the mind perceives everything as the present and will not make this distinction for you.

You always have the ability to determine your future if you are willing and able to look at your past. If this seems scary, remember the past does not really exist anymore. It is simply a thought that you carry in your mind. The memory of eating breakfast this morning is as distant as the Persian war. They are both in the past and do not really exist anymore.

In parenting, linking offers tremendous application. When you realize you have not handled a particular interaction well with your child, you have the ability to time travel and link. Your brain can go back to the past to develop the insight to where you have been previously. Perhaps a particular behavior, such as lying, sends your nervous system into overdrive. Being a mindful parent allows you to link your past experience to the present moment and create a new future by imagining yourself responding from a place of love the next time. You do not have to recreate the past. The past is the past. Let your mind know it is the past so you have the consciousness to create a new future. While it may seem difficult at first, it truly is possible to change your future. It takes a willingness to be honest in your time travel and the intention, commitment, desire, and follow-through at a high level of consciousness to make the changes in the future. It takes being present.

Calming the Amygdala. The amygdala is the fear receptor in the brain. It monitors perceptual input and is constantly on-guard for life-threatening stimuli. For individuals with perpetual trauma histories, their amygdala is trained to "watch-out' constantly, even during normal life situations. The result is an overly active amygdala, which is exhausting to the body system. The amygdala is also linked to the autonomic nervous system which is linked to the stress response system. If the inhibitory fibers in the brain are underdeveloped, shutting down this stress response system is difficult. Brain science now shows us that healing from trauma can actually promote growth of these inhibitory fibers, allowing the brain to shift back to a state of equilibrium, instead of being on alert 24 hours a day.[5] Additionally, when the amygdala fires intensely, it can literally shut down the neocortex. Your ability to think logically and make rational decisions is severely compromised.

Calming the amygdala takes a commitment to mindfulness, especially for parents with trauma histories themselves. For such parents, their amygdala is more easily activated, thus they are typically more easily angered, have less patience, and are living at a high stress level. Combine this with a child with the same characteristics and what is the result? Explosions! You have a parent-child relationship that is volatile, tense, and in need of connection.

If this sounds familiar to you, it will take mindfulness to not let the fear get ahead of you. Stay connected to first yourself and with what is "bubbling up" inside of you. Stay attuned to your child's emotional state. When you sense a shift in your child's state of regulation, move in closer in a proactive way to help soothe his activated amygdala. The more you can create an environment of safety, trust, and predictability, the more you are helping your child's amygdala to reset itself – you're resetting the thermostat. It does take repetition of these calming experiences but the great news is that repair is possible. Our bodies have the capacity for healing...it just takes the safety of love, understanding, reassurance through relationships, and repetition, repetition, repetition.

Your Gut Instinct. Being present puts you in touch with your intuition, your "gut instinct." From a psychological standpoint, intuition is a knowing, a sensing beyond the conscious understanding – a gut feeling. [6] Neurologically, intuition is the way you interpret the neuro-network of information that processes around the intestine and the heart (also known as the neuro-mechanisms).[7] We have networks around these areas that constantly process information. This information is sent upward through the spinal cord and ultimately to the neocortex of the brain. This neuro-network of information serves as a source of wisdom we call intuition. It is the most perfect form of "you."

This neurological explanation tells us that our bodies are equipped to give us the wisdom we need as parents. If a therapist recommends a technique that just does not feel right to you, then trust your gut. If a teacher is recommending a particular technique and your stomach turns, trust your gut. If your pediatrician is recommending a particular treatment or procedure and you feel uneasy about it, trust your gut. While professionals are doing the best they can, what they are recommending for your particular child may not always be the best. Do not lose your personal power to someone in authority. You are the parent and you know your child best. Tap into your intuition, your gut... you are equipped with a neuro-network of information to guide you in your parenting decisions. When you are present in the moment, free from fear, your gut instincts will be right on target.

The starting point is in you becoming mindful and learning to live in the present moment. The present moment is all you ever have. As Eckhart Tolle states, "There is never a time when your life is not 'this moment.'"[8] The past is the past and only exists as a memory in your mind. The future is only a thought in your mind; it is never a reality. Nothing can ever happen in the past and nothing can ever happen in the future. Life only happens in the present moment, and your children need you in the now.

To live in this moment, it takes loving yourself and accepting yourself at a deeper level than you have ever been able to do in the past. It takes going beyond just being comfortable in your own skin but becoming your own best friend. Developing this loving and healthy relationship with yourself is the key to developing a healthy relationship with your child. You will be opening up the space within you to be present with your child, which will simultaneously be creating the exact environment he needs to change his brain, his mind, his heart, and ultimately his behavior.

CHAPTER FOUR

Our Parenting Programs

■

"You can chain me, you can torture me,
you can even destroy this body,
but you will never imprison my mind."
– Mahatma Gandhi

It has been said that the mind is like a computer. As children, we install our "software" from our parents in the computers of our minds. We become programmed from our early childhood experiences. We gain an understanding of character, values, morals, and ethics from our parents. Yet more importantly, our parents model relationships to us. How we are parented is like a "program" embedded in our subconscious mind which, in turn, determines how we will parent our own children and form relationships with them. As children, we do not have the wisdom to determine whether or not these relational programs are functional, so all of our experiences with our parents become part of our make-up and part of our programming.

Conditional Love and Negative Messages. Unfortunately, many parents are not secure in who they are and do not embody self-love, self-worth, or self-esteem; they are not self-validating individuals. Hence, they seek these from their spouse and from their children. Their interpretation becomes, *"The better behaved my child is, the better I am as a parent."* The ability for the parent to feel good about himself then depends on the child's behavior. This sense of the parent needing to receive love and validation from the child leaves a program of conditional love instead of a program of unconditional love within the child. Love is not given freely. The love given by the parent requires that the child give back in the form of good behavior.

This dynamic is true for a majority of parents, if not at a conscious level, then all too often at the subconscious level. The percentage of parents who grew up in functional families, without this dynamic but with an atmosphere of true unconditional love, is small. While a statistic may be impossible to measure accurately, my estimate would be less than 10 percent of parents grew up in an atmosphere of unconditional love. At lectures with parents, I routinely ask about their families of origin and have them raise their hands if they grew up with parents who loved them unconditionally, with parents who could apologize to them, and with parents who could handle their level of emotional distress. In audiences of 150 parents, less than 15 parents will typically raise their hands.

Most of us grew up in negative, limiting environments. It has been calculated that by the time children are 8 years old, they have heard negative messages, with "no" being the central theme, about 50,000 times.[1] *"No, you can't have that." "No, you can't do that." "No, I can't buy that for you."* Every one of these messages created a neuro-pattern in the brain. The more you heard such negative messages from your parents, teachers, siblings, or from what you read or saw, the more these patterns became reinforced, developing an entire neuro-network of negativity in your brain. The more you received these negative messages, the stronger this neuro-network became within you.

In contrast, by the time children are 8 years old, they have only heard positive "yes" messages approximately 7,000 times.[2] That equates to more than seven times more negative messages than positive messages. Imagine your brain has seven times more negative neuro-patterns than positive ones. For many of us who grew up in intensely dysregulated families, these statistics are even more severe.

Childhood Programming. John Bowlby, the "Father of Attachment," stated over 50 years ago that "the first three years of our lives establishes the blueprints for all of our future relationships." He discovered this by studying and observing children's attachment behaviors. Science now brings further understanding to this statement. Brain science shows us that within the first two years of a child's life, the brain experiences the most rapid rate of growth in a person's entire lifespan.[3]

Dr. Bruce Lipton, a cellular biologist, describes one of the most memorable breakthroughs in his work was when he realized that the functioning of an individual human cell is similar to that of a personal computer. He writes of his excitement that cells are programmable, just like a computer. This programming for our cells comes not from genetics but from our external environment. Our environments program us down to the cellular level. The excitement of this realization was that it shed new light on modern science that left our programming up to heredity and genetics.[4] The magnitude of this is that we are not born victims to our genetic makeup.

But even with that liberating truth, you are thinking, *"GREAT! I'm free from my genetics, but what about my childhood programming? I'm from a completely dysfunctional family...now what do I do? My family didn't give me functional programming...I'm walking around with corrupt software, trying to parent a child with corrupt software, as well!"*

This is the pivotal understanding we must face in our lives as parents. Perhaps as a parent, it feels like you are working to create a castle in the sky within your family yet you are working from the blueprints of a shack. How do you get from picture "A" to picture "B?"

"A"   "B"

The good news is that you do not have to be a victim to these early life experiences. You have the opportunity to create new, life-giving, positive parenting programs that will become your family legacy for generations to come. You can move out of this place of victimhood because your brain is ever changing. Neuro-plasticity tells us we have the ability to continually formulate new connections, new programs. We used to think we were hard-wired at birth and we simply had to accept what we were given from our genetics. However, brain scan imaging shows us we can actually create new connections all the time. At this very moment, your brain is making a million connections a second.

The Brain. The brain has two main responsibilities. If you are raising a traumatized child who lives in survival mode, you are already quite familiar with the first responsibility: to sustain life. At a primal level, the brain will do whatever it takes to stay alive. Second, your brain has the responsibility to make certain that your outside environment matches up or correlates with the internal neuron patterns of your brain. If negative patterns are within, the brain will seek to create the same in your external environment. In other words, the outside has to match the inside.

This is the reason why a child who was raised in a chaotic and stressful home continues to attempt to create chaos and stress when placed in a stable, loving, and predictable home. His neuro-circuitry is programmed in the old ways and his system is working to match and create the same externally as what is patterned within him internally. It will take new experiences, within the context of safe and nurturing relationships to reprogram his programs.

So to help change your child's subconscious neuro-network, it takes changing your programming first. The more you can stay regulated in the face a dysregulated child, the easier your child's neuro-circuitry will be rewired. Conversely, if you react in fear – yelling, screaming, demanding, giving parental consequences that add more stress, or emotionally abandoning him – there is nothing within your child's environment to initiate change. The negative cycling between you will continue.

Your child's actions are being driven by patterns and programs laid down within his neurological system. It is not about will power or making a better choice. Yet, your child's negative programming can be rewritten through his relationship with you.

Cellular Survival. At a cellular level, Dr. Bruce Lipton describes how individual cells are literally programmed for survival. When individual human cells are placed in a Petri dish, they will actively avoid anything toxic or threatening to their survival.[5] These cells in the Petri dish are representative of how we act as human beings because we are simply active communities of more than 50 trillion individual cells. Are there not times as a parent when you seek distance from your child, avoiding him at all costs, not even wanting him to come home from school, just like the cell in the Petri dish?

In a research study I conducted with adoptive mothers raising challenging children, 93 percent of them stated there were many times they simply wanted to get in their cars and drive away, forever![6] That is 93 percent who had reached their state of survival and felt the urge from within to leave and avoid the toxic relationship going on between her and her child. Do you fall in this 93 percent?

Who's In the Driver's Seat? Have you ever woken up in the morning and said to yourself, *"Today I'm going to be different with my child. I'm going to exercise patience, work to create understanding, and respond instead of react."* Then, in less than 10 minutes, you find yourself frustrated, yelling, and completely reactive? It is not that you are not trying hard enough – it is because you are only working at the conscious level, and all the while your subconscious is the real bus driver, taking you off your new path without you even knowing it. Your subconscious programming will revert to old ways of thinking. Aligning both the conscious and the subconscious to a common goal takes mental conditioning. It takes retraining your mind; essentially, it takes reprogramming your previous programming.

In *Beyond Consequences, Logic, and Control,* Volume 1, the "bottom file drawer" was discussed. The bottom file drawer is your deepest level of memory. It is where traumatic memories and unprocessed feelings are buried, deep in the subconscious. When you get stressed out and overwhelmed, you shift into survival and work from these programs to protect yourself from harm.

The mind assumes everything is happening in the present.[7] When a Vietnam veteran with unresolved trauma walks through a parking lot and hears a car backfire, he shudders and squats down to protect himself. It is as if he is back in the war zone. His mind connects all his experiences to the present moment. Dr. Bruce Perry's research explains that the reptilian brain and the limbic brain initiate responses before the neo-cortex can interpret it and, as in this example, contextualize the sound, resulting in an exaggerated startle response.[8] This is the concept of linking, as discussed in the previous chapter. It takes being mindful to separate the past from the present so the two experiences do not merge as one.

This same concept is evident when parents find themselves having difficulties staying calm and regulated with their children. For example, if you are seeking to get your child's attention and have him respond to you, yet he ignores you, your mind can connect this moment with a scenario similar to one in your past. Perhaps as a child you could not get your mother's attention, so now when faced with a child whose attention you cannot obtain, you react strongly to him. This kind of exaggerated response is an indication of you reacting out of the past. Your mind is linking everything to the present. Your mind cannot recognize the past and cannot separate the two events. They are linked as one and the same.

To create the distinction between the past and the present, it takes making the separation at a conscious level and describing it as the past. It would simply take you saying to yourself, "This is my son, not my mother. I'm not a helpless child anymore. I'm okay." You have the ability to change the way you experience the present, despite anything that has happened in the past. It takes awareness, mindfulness and the courage to break the fear barrier. Bonnie Harris, author of *When Your Kids Push Your Buttons,* beautifully reminds us that "when fear gets in the way of self-change, it keeps us from connecting with our heart." Change requires you being in the driver's seat and finding the courage to take charge of your mind.

Liberation. At a certain point, the information we gather at the conscious level is transferred to the subconscious. It is like learning to drive. At first there is a conscious effort involved and, as you repeat this pattern over and over daily, the experience goes from conscious thought to subconscious memory. The conscious awareness then becomes a subconscious skill. Think about how many times you either drove to work or drove to go pick up your children and thought, "Umm, how did I get here?" You do not have to think at a conscious level about how to drive anymore.

It is estimated that 96 percent of your perceptions in a day are subconscious – unless you are taking action to create within yourself a higher level of consciousness. When we are not living at a high level of awareness, we simply shift into autopilot, doing the same thing today we did yesterday. We live out of the subconscious programs already established within us. For most of us, our automatic parenting programs are not conducive to reducing the fear and overwhelm in our children. We continue in the same way, day after day, feeding the negative neurological feedback loops within our families, simply wishing it was better (see *Beyond Consequences, Logic, and Control,* Volume 1, for more information on negative neurological feedback loops).

Creating new programs within us, free of fear and reactivity towards our children's defiant behaviors, takes creating new subconscious programs within us. The way we perceive and respond (or react) to an event or crisis is largely responsible for the ultimate outcome of that event. If we can understand and make sense out of an event, relate to our child's fear, stop taking it personally, and come to an objective conclusion from it, we have the ability to stay in a place of love. Just imagine what it would be like every time your child lied to you or gave you a *"Whatever!"* and you were able to automatically, from a subconscious level, stay regulated and remain in an understanding and loving state. Instead of a trigger reaction you had to fight and overcome, a loving response would come with ease and comfort.

As a parent, you can be a master at taking control of your mind. You can diminish the neuro-programs in your mind that are creating barriers to your ability to stay regulated and connected with your child. It takes learning how to take action and controlling your mind. I am certain that you have, in the past, sabotaged yourself and lost control of your parental responses, later to ask yourself, *"What was I thinking?"* You weren't thinking. You allowed yourself to go into autopilot, and your subconscious programming took over.

You no longer have to accept the negative thoughts and programming you absorbed as a child. These do not work for you anymore, and they certainly are not working for you in your relationship with your child. **Beliefs are nothing more than feelings of certainty based on your experiences or what somebody told you;** you always have the opportunity to create new positive beliefs within yourself and programs that work for your life. Ask yourself these questions:

1. "Whose life am I living...my thoughts and beliefs or somebody else's?"
2. "Am I going to accept the limitations and the false interpretations put on me, or am I going to take a different path to happiness, harmony, peace, and love?"
3. "Am I going to choose the path of the victim who suffers and struggles, or am I going to choose the path of transformation to be the best parent I can be?"

It takes training yourself just as you would train to run a marathon. It takes self-discipline and self-awareness to tap into the power within yourself. It starts with your thoughts because your thoughts do matter. Your thoughts create your reality. You have to choose the positive thoughts to be a different parent and to love your children during disruptive behaviors. Negative thoughts have been created in the past due to a simple lack of understanding and interpretations based out of fear.

■

Your thoughts create your reality.

■

When something is outside our understanding, we inevitably view it as abnormal or negative. If you do not understand your child's behavior, you will automatically view your child through a negative lens. To change, it takes a new understanding. It takes loving your child enough to walk in his shoes and see it from his perspective. The truth is that when you can understand your child from your child's point of view, his behavior actually will be quite logical. In the past we have forgotten in the past to ask the question, *"Who's defining the logic here?"* We assumed our logic was the only logic. The *Beyond Consequences* parenting paradigm will allow you to see that what your child is doing is, actually, quite logical.

To make permanent changes in your programs, thoughts, perspectives, and responses, it takes intention, commitment, desire, and most importantly, follow through. If your programs are buried deep, it takes you demanding more of yourself and making change happen, without fail. On a broader spectrum, it is your responsibility as a parent to stop any negative programming that has been a part of your family for generations in order not to hand this down to your children. Your work today has the ability to change future generations.

It is Up to You. The most important concept to accept is that nobody is going to make it work for you except for you. Changing your programming from the past is now your personal responsibility. Personal peace, validation, acceptance from within cannot come from an outside source and it cannot come from your children. It takes forgiveness of those who hurt you in your past and it takes loving yourself fully and completely, despite your past experiences. Love and acceptance of who you are is your responsibility. It is about you becoming your own best friend. This then equips you to keep unveiling the mask of anger, façade of disrespect, and coating of manipulation your children present to you daily. What your children present to you is really an illusion. Behind the anger, behind the disrespect, and behind the manipulation is a scared child in desperate need of connection, love, and acceptance.

> ■
> *What your children present to you is really an illusion. Behind the anger, behind the disrespect, and behind the manipulation is a scared child in desperate need of connection, love, and acceptance.*
> ■

When you are loving yourself and no longer depending on your children for validation, you can then be in a place where you are unshakable.

No matter what behaviors they present, you will be able to lift the behavioral veil to see their truth of internal fear, and in many cases, terror.

How to make this change in yourself is going to be your personal journey. It might take journaling, therapy, self-help books, audios, live workshops, DVD's, support groups, and reading and re-reading this book. It is imperative you work at the three dimensional levels in your life to create transformation and put you in a regulated, balanced place. This means working at the body, mind, and spirit levels together.

Affirmations. Affirmations are an amazingly effective way to re-program yourself. They are software for your mind. If you have never used affirmations or have had a negative opinion of them, below is an example to try. It is an affirmation especially designed to help you in your relationship with yourself and your children. Use this affirmation, or one you create, as a way to update and revise your current software. *(Now, don't skip to the next chapter; give it a try!)*

> *I recognize now, that I need to take back control of my life. I know full well that I have the right and the responsibility to make my life work for me now. And I accept that now.*
>
> *I am 100 percent committed to accepting myself as a viable power within my life. I refuse to give my personal power away and I accept that now. I know full well it is my responsibility to reclaim my personal power and I am doing that now.*
>
> *I know now that I can handle any situation effectively and efficiently with love, patience, and tolerance. I know full well that I have the ability to remain in a state of love, under all conditions, all circumstances, and at all times. I accept that now.*
>
> *I refuse to allow negative behaviors or negative reactions of others to influence me. I accept that now. Negative reactions of my children will bounce off me, because I am confident in who I am, and I am committed to loving myself fully and completely. I accept that now.*
>
> *I can stand face to face with negative behaviors, knowing full well that these behaviors come from fear and stress. I refuse to believe that my child's negativity is an indication of my ineffectiveness. I accept that now.*

I refuse to buy into the fear and false interpretations I've had in the past of being an ineffective parent or being an ineffective individual. I am loving myself, accepting myself, and I am respecting myself. I know I can do that now. I am doing that now.

I am loving and forgiving myself for allowing myself to slide backwards and for allowing myself to lose myself in the midst of stressful situations. I know now that I wasn't taking responsibility and that I was blaming others for my inability to be alright. I accept that now.

I know now that I rejected myself in the past, telling myself "I'm not alright" and "I'm not acceptable." And "I can't do this." But I know now, I'm perfectly alright, perfectly acceptable, and perfectly capable. I am accepting that now. And I'm doing that now.

I know now it is my responsibility to make my life work for me, regardless of what has happened in the past and regardless of the stress and fear present in my family now. I know now that it starts with me. I know that freedom from this bondage begins with me, and I accept that now.

I know now that liberation begins with my own self-love and I accept that now. I am releasing myself from the bondage of the past. I know now that it is my responsibility to love and forgive myself. I'm 100 percent committed to accepting myself and loving myself. I am doing that now. I am entitled to love, happiness, and abundance, and I accept my own entitlement. I am loving myself, accepting and forgiving myself. I am reclaiming and embracing myself. I am doing that now.

I am loving and forgiving all those in my life who were unable to love me and accept me the way I needed them to. I am doing that now. I am loving and forgiving myself, knowing full well that I am alright. I've always been alright. I accept myself fully and completely, and I am doing that now.

New Responses. By reprogramming your programming, you will be able to respond to your child instead of react to him. It will afford you more patience and more understanding – essentially more love. You will have more space between the stimuli and the response. The old fear-based reactions that produced disconnect and separation will be of the past. The old programs that resulted in strained relationships filled with anger, anxiety, grief, and resentment will be replaced by positive love-based programs, allowing you to have responses of forgiveness, acceptance, acknowledgement, validation, understanding, tolerance, assurance, and affection. Table 4.1 below illustrates the stark contrast between the two.

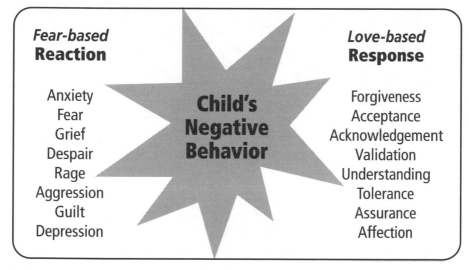

Figure 4.1

Commit to spending time each day working on your mind, along with being mindful of canceling out any negative self-talk. Following through with this can have magical effects on your regulatory ability. The sky's the limit when it comes to creating positive affirmations for yourself. Love yourself enough to try it and see the results magnify in peace, happiness, and joy in your life.

CHAPTER FIVE

Window of Stress Tolerance
∎

"Stress is the spice of life."
– Hans Selye

Stress is essential to our existence. Without it, we would live in a dreaded state of boredom and in fact, "complete freedom from stress is death."[1] There are two sides to stress, each opposite from the other. "Eustress" refers to stress that is healthy, positive, and constructive. Eustress stimulates growth and creativity. It drives us to take action in our lives and keeps us moving forward instead of stagnating. "Distress," on the other hand, is damaging or unpleasant stress. Distress is an overabundance of stress that causes us to deviate from our normal behavior. It is persistent stress that stays with us, unresolved and overwhelming. Distress causes discomfort. It can lead to anxiety and depression because it creates an awareness of helplessness and imperfection.

Dr. Hans Selye, an Austrian-born physician, first introduced the concept of stress to the field of mental health in 1936. He defined stress as "the nonspecific response of the body to any demand made upon it"[2] In other words, he was stating that our bodies respond in some way when experiencing stress. The amount of stress we can handle in a positive way is our "window of stress tolerance." Once we hit our breaking point, we are outside our window of stress tolerance.

For many children with difficult and severe behaviors, they live in a perpetual state of distress. Their high level of stress distorts their perception of the world and keeps them living in a state of fear. With this understanding, it becomes clear that in actuality, their behaviors are perfectly normal – normal considering their internal state of distress. It is just that it is **their** normal, not our normal.

Unfortunately, we consider these behaviors abnormal because we compare them to the behaviors of children who are living at a comfortable level of eustress. Children in a state of eustress have a large window of stress tolerance. They have the capacity to think clearly, to reciprocate love and kindness, and to be respectful of others around them. We have learned to call this group of well-behaved children "normal" and the other group "abnormal." Yet, this is judgmental and offers no understanding of the state of internal stress of these children's reality.

The following graphic illustrates this principle. The light gray area represents the level of stress the child (we will call him Andy) operates out of on a daily basis. On a scale of zero to 100, where 100 is the point where Andy would hit his breaking point, we see that he lives at a mild level of stress of about 20. The dark gray area from 20 to 100 represents Andy's window of stress tolerance. This means that Andy has a large window to handle stressful events that come his way. He has a long way until he hits his breaking point.

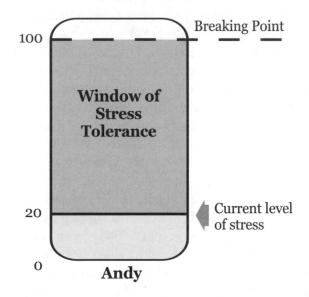

Andy has been living in a loving, nurturing, safe, and predictable environment for the first eight years of his life. In fact, his womb experience was even ideal. His mother was in a loving place emotionally, had planned the pregnancy, took care of herself, and was supported by her husband. Andy has been bathed in unconditional love, he feels accepted and loved, and he has been supported through difficult times. So, Andy lives at a low level of stress, giving him a large space between his current level of stress and his breaking point.

The next graph illustrates a child who is the exact opposite. This child (let us call him Bobby) had life-threatening experiences in the womb. His mother was being abused by her husband, both physically and emotionally. Bobby's parents divorced when he was 6 months old, which left him being raised by a young single mother struggling to make ends meet. He was in and out of different daycares and at 2 years old, his mother hit rock bottom and left him for two days in a hotel while she worked the streets. Children and Family Services took Bobby from his mother and he lived in six different foster homes for the next four years until Bobby was placed with his aunt and uncle. He has scheduled visitations with his mother but she is unpredictable in making it to these visits. At 8 years old, Bobby's current stress level on this stress scale is an 80 out of 100.

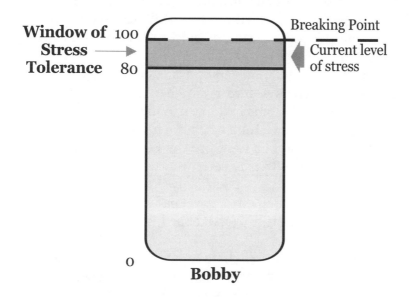

Consider the difference between these two children, both age 8, yet each with a significantly different window of stress tolerance. Andy is a child who has a tremendous amount of flexibility. He can handle stressful situations. When his toy breaks or he cannot find his favorite shirt, he may get upset but he does not collapse into an emotional abyss. Bobby, on the other hand, has no flexibility and when he wakes up expecting to eat his favorite cereal for breakfast then finds out the box is empty, he flies into a rage. Bobby has no tolerance for stress, slips into overwhelm easily, and crumbles emotionally at the slightest event in his life.

Traditionally, we have viewed these children as either good or bad. Our perspective of them has been based solely on an external symptom – their behavior. Yet in reality, a child's behavior is a only a symptom or a by-product of his internal state of regulation or

■

A child's behavior is only a symptom or a by-product of his internal state of regulation or dysregulation.

■

dysregulation. This internal state of regulation determines the size of a child's window of stress tolerance. We need to stop judging children as being "good" or "bad" but view them as either "regulated" or "dysregulated." This terminology is congruent with their window of stress tolerance and more importantly, it removes the negativity placed on children who are unable to regulate during stressful times. Describing children as regulated or dysregulated implies that it is simply a state in which they can toggle back and forth. Naming children as dysregulated, versus "bad," affords them the opportunity to be seen as able to become regulated without barriers or limitations.

Relate the concept of regulation versus dysregulation to your own experiences. There have been days in your life where nothing seems to go right. After awhile, you become irritable and the littlest things seem unmanageable. Or think of a time when you had only a few hours of sleep one night. The next day you were tired and dysregulated. You were quick to snap at people and easily became upset. Your window of stress tolerance was small due to a physical body that was stressed out and sleep deprived. Were you good one day yet bad the next? No, you were simply dysregulated and easily overwhelmed. You had a small window of stress tolerance.

Children need their parents to help to expand their window of stress tolerance. The parent-child relationship, according to Dr. Allan Shore, serves as the attachment mechanism, the dyadic regulation of emotion, to modulate positive emotional states as well as negative emotional states of children.[3] Through the relationship with the child, the parent becomes the regulator for the child. The key, however, lies within the parent's capacity to monitor and regulate her own emotional states, especially negative emotional states. As children are parented using a love-based paradigm (as demonstrated throughout this book) with parents who are regulated, calm, and responsive instead of reactive, authoritative, and emotionally void, their internal systems begin to calm down. Their windows of stress tolerance enlarge. They become more flexible and develop the capacity to handle difficult life situations with tolerance, patience, and adaptability.

Neuroscience explains this further. We have the ability to rewire our neurological connections, a healing process known as "neuroplasticity." Neuroplasticity enables healing from trauma and allows the body's response system to adjust to new experiences within the environment. Even as you are reading this page, your brain cells are making an average of one million new connections per second.[4] New experiences enhance neuroconnections in your brain.

As Bobby experiences more positive, nurturing, and emotionally safe experiences, he will be laying down new neuropathways. His response system will readjust in a calm and safe environment. Recently I had a mom come up to me at a lecture and give me an excellent example of this. Her son, exceptionally hyper-active, was prescribed ADHD medications and was struggling in school. As she became a Beyond Consequences parent, changing her parenting to this love-based model, within a short amount of time, her son was able to begin school with no medications and was earning A's and B's. First, this child's environment changed and, second, his relationship with his mother changed, resulting in his body system being able to expand its window of stress tolerance.

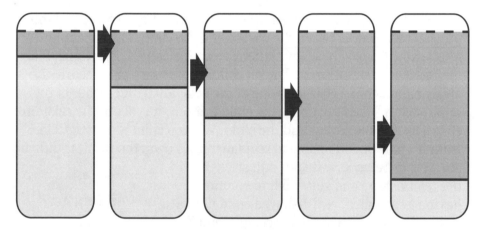

**Increasing a Child's Window of Stress Tolerance
Through Environment and Relationship**

Helping a child increase his window of stress tolerance comes through changing his environment and changing the interactions between his parents and other adults in his life. Sometimes children simply need their parents to make their worlds "small." This may require reducing the amount of after school activities. Instead of guitar on Monday, soccer on Tuesday, church on Wednesday, and martial arts on Thursday, the child may need to be home after-school each day with only one planned activity on Saturday. It might mean changing the child's classroom to a smaller classroom with a calmer and more regulated teacher. Perhaps it means being home schooled and staying in one environment during the day to give the child's system time to relax and find a better state of balance. Instead of going to Super Walmart, perhaps a short trip to the local Walgreens is all he can handle for the time being.

As the child's system is given a chance to settle down, he will be able to handle more activities and larger environments. It first takes meeting him at his window of stress tolerance and then helping him to increase and expand his life at a rate that fits his healing process. Many times it is the parent's fear that begins to push the child too fast. Children need to heal on their timing, not the parent's timing.

When a child is disconnected from his parent and unable to regulate on his own, the result is difficult and severe behaviors.

In addition to making modifications to a child's environment, it is imperative the healing process include interactive repair between the parent and the child. The parent-child relationship needs to be strengthened and developed. Dr. Daniel Siegel makes an important point that "in children, security or insecurity of attachment is not a characteristic of the individual, but rather of the relationship."[5] It is not about the child himself; it is about the relationship between the parent and the child. When a child is disconnected from his parent and unable to regulate on his own, the result is difficult and severe behaviors. Repair and strengthen the relationship and you will find solutions to having a regulated, well-behaved child with a large window of stress tolerance. As a child's window of stress tolerance increases, his ability to self-regulate increases, as well. It is through creating dependence between you and your child that you will foster independence and self-regulation in the future.

Children need to heal on their timing, not the parent's timing.

CHAPTER SIX

Expectations
■
"A thing long expected takes the form
of the unexpected when at last it comes."
– Mark Twain

One of the most common causes of conflict between a parent and his child is the result of expectations that are incongruent with the child's abilities and characteristics. While children need their parents to have expectations to help them achieve and accomplish greatness, expectations that do not address an individual child's regulatory abilities and innate qualities can lead to disastrous results. Ironically, it can be a parent's well-intended expectations that actually create unneeded conflict and stress and can become the direct cause of a child's under-achievement, lack of motivation, and overwhelm.

As parents, it is only natural to desire that our children have wonderful childhoods and grow up to have better lives than our own. After all, the basis of the American Dream is that anyone can achieve whatever is desired through hard work and perseverance. The very idea of telling someone to ease up on his dreams seems almost absurd. Yet, that is exactly what I am suggesting (at least temporarily) for some children.

Children with trauma histories have a high sensitivity to stress. Unfortunately, parental expectations can be the triggering sensory piece that heightens this level of stress. These parental expectations can increase a child's fear state and increase the child's state of overwhelm.

When children are not secure in their attachment relationships, they do not have a core understanding that they are safe and loved and that their behavior or performance has no bearing on them being accepted and loved by their parents. Children who have a history of loss, broken relationships, and painful experiences easily correlate their performance with their security. Their interpretation becomes, *"If I do well and please my parents, then I'm safe and secure."* The opposite side

■

Children who have had a history of loss, broken relationships, and painful experiences easily correlate their performance with their security.

■

of this same coin then says, *"If I don't do well and if I disappoint my parents, then I'm not safe and I am not loved."* For a child not to be loved, death is imminent. Children know on an intrinsic level that they cannot survive without love.

In an effort to avoid losing this love, children become so overwhelmed they simply cannot function under this amount of stress. Parents become frustrated and disappointed due to the child's unmet expectations. The child feels this increase in stress, regresses further from his developmental capabilities, and the negative neurological feedback loop is in full swing between parent and child. The parent's fear of the child not being a capable adult becomes knotted up with the child's fear of not being loved and accepted. The parent's fear of not being a good parent due to the performance of his child adds into this fear cycle. All these fears ping pong back and forth, breeding more and more fear into this already insecure relationship between the parent and the child.

Avoiding this cycle or putting an end to its viciousness becomes the parent's responsibility. Realigning parental expectations is an absolute necessity in finding peace in your home. These parental expectations originate from the following:

Cultural standards. Cultural norms and expectations at a macro scale often influence the expectations parents develop at the micro scale, within their own homes. General cultural standards give us a starting point, but if your child is not meeting these precisely, remember to stop and look at the individual child's characteristics before going to a place of panic and worry. Cultural standards are typically specific to that culture and are only based off of tradition, with no scientific proof and with little understanding of the child's individual needs or characteristics. For example, the standard IQ test is accepted as an accurate, scientific, and valuable tool to measure intelligence. However, this measurement tool ignores factors such as race/ethnicity and socio-economic status, which can have a significant effect on a child's IQ score. Additionally, the IQ test was set to the intelligence level of the left-brain thinker, offering little hope for a child who operates from predominately the right side of his brain. These factors can greatly skew the results of such a test and should not be held as an absolute indication of your child's intelligence.

Developmental standards. There is a plethora of parenting books listing developmental milestones for children of all ages (for example: *What to Expect in the Toddler Years*). While such information can be helpful to a certain point, these expectations may not apply to your individual child. These books are written according to a child's "chronological age," not the child's "emotional age." This is an important distinction. Many children with trauma histories are emotionally delayed in their development, so their emotional age is in conflict with their chronological age. For example, children who develop language skills behind their peers are often rushed into speech classes prematurely without considering this might add more stress to this particular child's individual development.

Your historical framework. Your own childhood experiences have created a framework that influences your present-day expectations of your child's abilities. Have you ever thought, *"I never would have acted this way when I was his age!"* or *"I certainly could pack my own lunch when I was 10 years old!"* What is important to remember is that a child's brain is an historical organ.[1] It remembers the past while concurrently, the child's nervous system is profoundly influenced by early life experiences. Your child is working from a different physical existence than you were; his behavior is going to be different from your behavior at that same age.

Comparison to other children his age. Within our social network of friends, we consciously and subconsciously compare our children with other children. When our children fail in comparison, we immediately go to a place of fear. We fear our children will not be alright and we fear that we are not good parents. The adage of comparing "apples to oranges" holds true in this situation. It is unfair to compare your child to another child who has had healthy, secure relationships and expect him to be as capable, responsive, and sensitive as this child.

Learning styles. There are four basic learning styles. These include visual, auditory, kinesthetic, and tactile. Visual learners learn best through looking at images, demonstrations, and body language. Auditory learning occurs through hearing the spoken word. Kinesthetic learning is learning through the act of doing and interacting. Tactile learners need to write notes and draw diagrams, as well as use touch, to learn.

If your child is a visual learner, giving instructions verbally may be the reason he does not follow through with the instructions and does not meet your expectations. Most young children learn best through kinesthetic and tactile approaches, so do not expect such children to be able to simply listen to a request and be able to comply. Tailoring your parental requests and expectations to your child's learning style will yield much better outcomes.

Personality type. The combination of the parent's personality type with the child's personality type can be a significant factor in children failing to meet their parents' expectations. We all have a different personality type. Becoming mindful of our own personality type and then identifying our child's personality type has the potential for opening up an incredible amount of emotional space and tolerance for our children.

In the mental health field, there are standard personality profiles such as the Myers-Briggs, Galen's four temperaments, and the Keirsey Temperament Sorter. These serve their purpose, but there is a wonderfully simple and fun way to identify personality types. It is a personality system that is simple and easy to remember without any studying. This personality profiles system was originally designed by Dr. Gary Smalley and Dr. John Trent. They based it around four animal characteristics. It is a classification system you can teach your children, which will in turn help them to relate to other people with more understanding and tolerance.

The four personality types they identified are the lion, otter, golden retriever, and beaver. These four animals are essentially all you have to know for this personality classification system:

> **Lions.** Lions are natural leaders. They are determined, bold, confident, and they take charge to make their lives work for them. They enjoy challenges and are great problem solvers. Weaknesses of the lion include being opinionated, arrogant, and unsympathetic. Children who are lions are easily bored and can be difficult to please. If you are raising a lion, he may need more of your help in learning compassion and tolerance.

> **Otters.** Otters are playful, carefree, and talkative. They like to be the center of attention in social situations, and they get along with almost anyone. They breed enthusiasm and live for the present moment. With these great qualities comes the flip side of being unpredictable, lacking in self-control, and being disorganized. They are easily distracted and, because they are so sociable, school work often becomes a low priority.

Beavers. Beavers pay attention to details and are self-disciplined, creative, and intellectual. They are sensitive, predictable, and orderly. They set a high standard of quality for everything they do. However, the need for perfectionism can cause them to be critical and they often fret needlessly over assignments and become easily stressed. They are prone to depression and moodiness.

Golden Retrievers. Golden Retrievers are the "sweethearts" of the four personality types. They are calm, dependable, and good-natured. Golden retrievers are generally easy to get along with and they are peace-loving diplomats. However, in the avoidance of conflict, they can be passive and unenthusiastic. They dislike change and prefer to be "homebodies." Academically, they only do what is required...they tend to be minimalists.

Most people are predominately one personality type with one secondary type. Identifying your child's personality type is important to setting expectations that are reasonable and compatible with his personality type. For instance, expecting your son who is primarily a lion to be as compassionate as his sister who is a golden retriever can lead to complete frustration. Expecting your otter to easily stay focused and not goof around at times when you need him to be serious will prove annoying. Your beaver will be able to keep his room neat while your otter will be challenged in this area. Expecting your golden retriever to be a high achiever and self-motivated is setting her up for failure. Your lion is going to have great difficulty with authority figures and will react more intensely when you implement controlling parental techniques than will your beaver.

Additionally, it is important to identify your personality type as the parent. A father who is primarily a lion, bold and likes to take charge, will naturally have a difficult time relating to his daughter who is an otter – playful, carefree, and lacking self-discipline. The mother who is a beaver, orderly and a hard worker, will find herself with little tolerance raising a son who is a golden retriever – unenthusiastic and a minimalist.

It takes an awareness of the differences in personality types for parents to relate more fully to their children. Identifying these natural personality types first in yourself and then in your children, while staying in a place of awareness of them, will give you the ability to understand and appreciate your children better. This will lead to a greater window of tolerance, fostering more patience and love within you for them.

Examine the expectations you have set for each of your children. Customize these expectations to take into account their emotional age, their predominate learning style, their regulatory ability, your own framework of experiences from your childhood, and their personality type. Each child is unique and one set of expectations does not fit all. When you can identify the specific characteristic of each of your children, celebrate their uniqueness, and then set expectations accordingly.

PART TWO

Seven Behaviors Rooted in Fear

Note: *All of the examples given in the next seven chapters represent true stories submitted to the author by parents who have implemented the Beyond Consequences principles.*

CHAPTER SEVEN

Poor Social Skills

■

*"A man's growth is seen in
the successive choirs of his friends."*
– Ralph Waldo Emerson

"She knows how she is supposed to act, but the minute she gets around her friends she acts crazy. In her efforts to make friends, she repels them!"

"I ask him how he is supposed to act and he can tell me, no problem. He knows better, so why isn't he doing it?"

"Suzy has no sense of personal space, interrupts constantly, and acts like an idiot once she is around her friends no matter how much I coach her!"

"I cringe every time I watch Danny play with his friends. He tries so hard and then when the other children ignore him or make fun of him, he fights back and becomes aggressive."

"My daughter never even attempts to join in with the other children. She isolates herself, just watches the other children, and then complains of how miserable and lonely she is."

Do any of these thoughts or comments sound like ones you have had about your child? It is a painful experience to be a parent and watch your child completely sabotage his social life. We want our children to be able to develop friendships and to be liked and accepted by their peers.

For many of us as parents, this desire stems from our own experiences as children when we were picked on, singled out, or rejected by our friends. Were you always the last one to be picked for the kickball team? Did your friends have sleepovers and not include you? When you see history repeating itself with your own child, it can be unbearable.

As human beings, we are designed to be in relationships with one another. It is in our biological programming to be connected. When we are missing this piece in our life with peers our age, it can literally be painful. Dr. Bruce Lipton, author of *The Biology of Belief,* speaks to the necessity of us living within a community. We are designed at a biological and cellular level to live in relationships.[1]

Science now brings us the understanding we need to move beyond the importance of the individual and need to focus on the importance of the community. British scientist Timothy Lenton has shown that evolution is more dependent on the interaction among species than it is on the interaction within a species.[2] Life is a matter of the fittest groups rather than the fittest individuals. It is in our relationships that life exists and that we live up to our fullest potential, not within our individual singular selves. Social skills are an absolute necessity.

We are designed to learn social skills as young children to then grow up and live abundant lives within the context of relationships. These social skills include helping, discussing, compromising, negotiating, stating feelings, desires, cooperating, taking turns, empathizing with others, and many more. When these skills are not understood and implemented, the social consequences can be immense for children.

Traditional View

Traditionally, programs and approaches to helping children learn social skills have been primarily cognitive and behavioral based. Social Skills Training (SST), for instance, is a form of behavior therapy used by teachers, therapists, and trainers to help children who have difficulties relating to their peers.[3] Such approaches have focused on behavioral changes with the use of instructions, coaching, feedback, behavior rehearsal, and modeling.

As with most behavioral techniques, the primary goal is to focus on facilitating the desirable behavior while simultaneously eliminating the undesirable behavior. The idea is first to help children understand why appropriate skills are important for them to think through their choices when interacting with other children. The National Association of School Psychologists recommends using primarily positive strategies when helping children. They then encourage the use of "punitive strategies" if the positive approach is unsuccessful and the behavior is of a serious and/or dangerous nature.[4]

When working with children to learn how to play and engage in groups, traditional social skills approaches are based on the premise that children must learn how to play by the rules and that they need to learn how to cooperate within an activity. This will then aid in acquiring the ability to do preplanning and to organize successful interactions with peers. The goal is for the child to take another child's perspective and to be able to negotiate, learning to be accountable for his own actions.

A New View
Fear is the Root. While these traditional approaches appear reasonable at first, when we consider the core emotional issues driving children's poor social skills, it becomes clear the Traditional View has missed a vital piece to truly helping children. Let's review the first two foundational principles of the *Beyond Consequences* paradigm (see *Beyond Consequences, Logic, and Control,* Volume 1):

1. All behavior arises from an unconscious, fear-based state of stress.
2. There are only two primary emotions: love and fear.

Negative behavior is a sign of a stressed-out child. A stressed child is not working from an emotional state of love; he is working from a framework of fear. Traditional approaches neglect to consider or incorporate this essential understanding. No matter how conscious or intentional a child's negative social interaction may appear, the reality is that the child is being driven from an unconscious place. The child is not aware of his behavior. Dr. Bruce Lipton reiterates this point when he writes, "The actions of the subconscious mind are reflexive in nature and are not governed by reason or thinking." [5] Your child's reactions are automatic and unintentional, not deliberate or malicious. To demonstrate how to help a child, we begin this chapter's example with Billy:

> *Your child's reactions are automatic and unintentional, not deliberate or malicious.*

> *Billy, 8 years old, is at a new restaurant with his family. He cannot sit still, he is laughing and talking in a loud voice, and he is leaning back in his chair. When dinner comes, his table manners are that of 2-year-old; he reaches over his sister to grab more rolls while inhaling his dinner.*

This is a child who has little awareness of the way he is acting.

Even though Billy has been through several sessions of Social Skills Training with his therapist (as described in the Traditional View), at this present moment it is as if this child was raised by wolves and never had a single table manner taught to him!

In his state of stress, Billy simply cannot access the logical thinking part of his brain. He is too overwhelmed emotionally and is operating from more of a primal place. The abundance of being in a stimulating environment such as a restaurant where Billy is feeling unsettled and scared (especially since this is a restaurant he has never visited) has him in a heightened state of arousal. Manners and social appropriateness are the last items on his agenda.

Billy is simply doing all he can to try to settle his system. He is using the food as a means to regulate his internal system. This is a common solution typical for all of us. We have all at one time or another overeaten and stuffed ourselves with enjoyable food that gave us pleasure to distract ourselves from the discomfort of being in a stressful state. Be honest with yourself. Did you ever gorge on ice cream, cookies, or potato chips when you were stressed out?

It is the parent's role in such an example to help Billy create an awareness of what has happened to him since coming to this restaurant. It is the parent's responsibility to help him learn to identify and regulate his stress. Directing him at this moment to "use his manners" would only create more stress and more overwhelm. Reminding him to "use his restaurant voice" would be ignoring Billy as an emotional being and would be responding to him as if he is a robot, not a little boy. Threatening Billy with "no dessert" unless he calms down would only keep Billy in his negative physiological loop. Billy does know how to behave. He simply cannot behave right now because he is too dysregulated. His knowledge of good behavior has been hijacked by his state of fear and overwhelm.

> ■
>
> *His knowledge of good behavior has been hijacked by his state of fear and overwhelm.*
>
> ■

The solution is to calm Billy down. Then, and only then, will he be able put his social training into action.

> *"Billy, how about you and I take a break from this for a moment and get some fresh air? Just for a minute…we'll come right back. I want to make sure you're okay, sweetheart." Mom doesn't mention his behavior for the moment. She reassures him that*

they will be returning to the table and she uses a soft tone and an endearing nickname (sweetheart). Mom is working to interrupt the negative loop Billy is caught in through her emotional attunement, not through behavioral directives.

As mom is able to use her relationship with Billy to attend to his emotional needs, Billy is learning the life lesson of how to regulate. Such interactions, repeated over time, will give Billy the experience to be stressed out and then return to a state of calm and peace. His ability to modulate this over-abundance of stress, without reverting to negative behaviors, will improve more and more as he has positive and nurturing experiences. These experiences are programming Billy to learn how to self-regulate. At this point in his development, he does not have the coping skills to do it on his own. The parent's calm and loving response is equipping him to be able to do it on his own in the future.

The Traumatized Child. Children with grossly underdeveloped social skills have become this way due to their previous experiences of being in relationships that have caused pain. Their histories of trauma cannot be minimized or underestimated.

Toxic care giving, in examples of abuse or neglect, affects the child's ability to regulate from a body level. Traumatic experiences short circuit the body's natural ability to regulate the body's response to stress and impedes the body's ability to return to a state of balance when triggered by stress. These experiences, left unchecked, leave the child in a hyper-aroused state of stress. In other words, the child is left in perpetual overdrive, unable to hit the brakes to slow down on his own.

When Billy, as in the example above, becomes stressed, his response is to go into overdrive. This is a learned automatic reaction due to his early life experiences. Expecting him to stop and think through his behaviors is beyond his capacity at this point in his development.

Parent-Child Social Skills Training. The minute a child is born, he begins learning social interaction skills. It is in the primal relationship with his mother that nature's social skills training course begins. Dr. Allan Schore, an expert in the field of affect regulation, describes that when the mother looks at the baby and the two of them connect through their facial expressions, the infant is learning to relate in the safety of this relationship. He also writes that when these interactions are not safe and when an infant misses out on these experiences, the child will grow up having difficulty interacting appropriately in relationships.[6] Daniel Goleman, author of *Social Intelligence,* writes:

> *"This parent-loop offers the central passageway for parents to help their children learn the ground rules for relationships – how to attend to another person, how to pace an interaction, how to engage in conversation, how to tune in to the other person's feelings, and how to manage your own feelings while you are engaged with someone else. These essential lessons lay the foundations for a competent social life."[7]*

The ability to feel with others, to sense non-verbal emotional signals, to listen with full receptivity, to understand another person's thoughts and intentions, and to care about another person's needs comes from "experiential knowledge." This experiential knowledge comes from having someone, such as a parent, interact with you at this emotional level. They cannot come from cognitive training, as suggested in the Traditional View. This is why parenting your child from a relational framework becomes a powerful force in helping your child develop effective social skills. Checking back in with Billy at the restaurant, let's see how mom responds to her stressed-out child:

> *"Wow, Billy, it's pretty loud and busy inside that restaurant, isn't it?" Billy wordlessly nods a "Yes." "Let's you and I take a break outside here and then we'll go back in when we feel calmer." Mom takes a few deep breaths and motions for Billy to sit down next to her. They sit for a few minutes, having a light conversation and a few laughs about the little bug crawling up the flowers they are sitting next to and then mom asks Billy, "You seem a lot calmer now, are you ready to go back inside?"*

Billy's mom is working to interact with Billy to provide safety and a calm presence in order for Billy to calm down. Her attunement to how he is feeling is giving him the experience of someone understanding his needs. She places the importance of her relationship with him over the importance of him being obedient and well mannered in the restaurant. Mom understands that once Billy is calm and regulated, he will then be able to demonstrate appropriate manners.

As they walk into the restaurant, Mom says to Billy, *"Now that we're back inside, how about we both use our 'restaurant voices' and our good manners at the table?"* Billy nods his head and sits back down to finish his dinner in a way that even Ms. Manners would applaud. Billy is now able to use his social skills because he is calm enough to think clearly.

Self-esteem and Social Skills. Research has shown that a child's level of self-esteem directly influences the child's ability to socially engage in appropriate ways.[8] In other words, a child with low self-esteem is typically a child with poor social skills. A child with low self-esteem easily becomes an outcast in social situations and has difficulty relating to his peers because of two basic factors:

1. His lack of emotional regulation.
2. His status at the bottom of the social totem pole simply invites rejection and being picked on by his peers.

Additionally, Bowlby's work suggests that children with low self-esteem seek out peers who will confirm their low sense of self – a self-fulfilling prophecy of sorts.[9] Some children will go as far as to invite negative interactions, whereas Johnny will say to a bully, *"Aren't you going to tease me today? I promise I won't get mad."*

It is the parent's responsibility to help develop the child's emotional regulatory ability and to help build the child's self-esteem. Simply sending a child out into the middle of a playground to "figure it out" on his own will only create more of the same – a child who is even more dysregulated and a child who is reinforcing his belief that he is not lovable as he continues to be rejected by his own peers.

Research reinforces the significance of this parent-child relationship in preparation for peer relationships. It has been shown that when children have feelings of trust and security in the parent-child relationship, they have a higher level of self-esteem.[10] When children, boys in particular, felt controlled and dominated by the parent, they had lower self-esteem levels. This research is reinforcing that the level of self-worth children have with their peers is directly influenced by the parent-child relationship.[11] This is significant to the way in which children need to be parented for them to succeed in their relationships

■

The level of self-worth children have with their peers is directly influenced by the parent-child relationship.

■

outside the home.

Parenting from the *Beyond Consequences* paradigm, where the child is taught to self-regulate through a safe and loving relationship with the parent(s) and where the child is accepted unconditionally, will equip a child for a lifetime of successful social interactions. One mother's story locks this in beautifully:

> *My daughter, at age 8, was a complete outcast with her peers. When she wasn't being picked on, she would isolate herself in the far corner of the playground, playing and talking to herself. After six years of parenting her through this love-based paradigm, I found myself in tears of joy when I had a conference with her teacher. I asked the teacher how she was doing socially and he replied, "It is amazing. She is liked by everybody. We had an awards ceremony last week. When your daughter was recognized for her efforts on the basketball team, she received the loudest 'roar,' not once, but twice – louder than any of the other students. She has an uncanny ability to relate to all the students and to all the social clicks in her grade. That is rare for a middle schooler."*

Consider Your Child's Emotional Age. Children learn social skills with age. If you have a child whose emotional age is less than his chronological age, he will most likely have difficulty connecting with peers in the same grade level. For instance, let's say that your child is 8 years old, yet he is emotionally and socially more the level of a 5 or 6 year old. That would be like putting a kindergartener in with a group of third graders. He would get eaten alive! He simply doesn't have the skills to relate on the same level.

There are three basic categories of social skills children learn as they develop: physical, verbal, and thinking. Review the chart on pages 58-59 to see if your child's social behaviors are reflective of the examples given. Notice the other children in his playgroup or in his classroom and see if they are having the same difficulties as your child. If your child is the minority, then he is more emotionally immature than his peers and needs more time to master these social skills.

If your child is emotionally 5 and you are expecting him to behave like a 7-year- old, your expectation is unfair to his ability. It is overwhelming and scary for a child to be emotionally 5 and be expected to interact appropriately with older children. This fear is the root cause of many children's aggressive social behaviors. The child becomes so overwhelmed that he goes into "fight" mode and attacks.

> *Sandy was with her mom at a playgroup in the local Burger King's children's area. When Sandy was in a closed area with the other girls, she became verbally aggressive and began biting the other children.*

Traditionally, the caretaker would pull Sandy out and lecture her about not biting and perhaps put her in a time-out. With the *Beyond Consequences* approach, we now recognize that Sandy is feeling overwhelmed and very scared. An attacking behavior such as biting is a clear indication of a child who is feeling threatened. Sandy needs the adult in her life to acknowledge her fear instead of lecturing her about appropriate behavior.

> *Sandy's mom comes over and picks her up. She takes Sandy to a quieter place in the restaurant and reassures Sandy that she will be okay. Mom says, "Sandy, it looks like you got really scared with the other girls. I'm sorry you felt so unsafe, sweetheart." Mom holds Sandy and rocks her gently. Once Sandy is calm, Mom asks Sandy if she is ready to go back and play. This gives Sandy the chance to set her own limits and begin the process of self-awareness. Yet before Sandy jumps into the middle of the play area, Mom says to Sandy, "If you get scared again, just come get me so I can keep you safe. I'll be right over on that bench."*

This gives Sandy an alternative to biting. If Sandy's mother notices this behavior happens frequently, she should set-up play dates with younger children. Younger children would give Sandy the opportunity to play with children more her emotional age, giving her a safer environment in which to develop her social skills. With enough repetition and loving support, Sandy will advance her social age to meet her chronological age.

Provide a Regulated Environment. Children need to learn to play and interact in a regulated and safe environment. In the example with Sandy, her mom let her know that she would be right there if she needed her help. Children need an adult either right there during the social exchange (in cases where the child is overly stressed and scared) or in close proximity. The adult provides a "safe base" for a child and creates a level of safety he does not have on his own.

It is similar to the behavior of a typical 2-year-old. At 2 years old, a toddler begins to separate from his caretaker and runs off to explore his environment. He then comes back within a short time to reconnect with his mommy or daddy. He is coming back, seeking safety and regulation. Eventually, the time he can stay away from the parent lengthens and he develops the ability to self-regulate and feel safe on his own.

Applying this same instinctual process when your child is playing with another child, it is important for you to be nearby, to be attuned, and to be attentive to what is happening with the two children. Allow some space for the child to work through challenges, but come in and be part of the play to keep the situation from snowballing out of control, if needed.

A more proactive approach would be to systematically come in and check in with your child every 10 or 15 minutes. *"Hi, Richey. Just making sure you're all right. Okay, glad you and Jimmy are having fun. Come get me if you need me. I'll be right next door in the living room."*

Social interactions are stressful for children; play is their work. Interrupt the play experience with quick visits to reconnect and to help regulate your child. Offer a snack, suggest a new game or a change in environment such as going outside, and limit the time of the play in the beginning until you have a better understanding of your child's window of stress tolerance.

In the beginning, it may not be in your child's best interest to go to another child's home to play without you. A new environment can be too overwhelming and scary. Instead of dropping off your child, stay with him and visit with the parent. Be available if your child needs you.

This is especially true for group gatherings such as birthday parties. Do not leave your child alone until you are certain he is ready, even if you are the only parent there. It is more important for you to create safety for your child so he learns to handle such events on his own in the future. Risk looking like the "overbearing parent." Most parents have no framework to understand that you are staying for your child's sake and many parents may conclude you are having issues letting your child grow up. Stay confident in knowing you are providing exactly what your child needs and simply say to the parent host, "I'd like to stay just so I know that Jenny is okay and doesn't get too overwhelmed with all the excitement and fun."

Outside Social Play. Playing outside can be a stimulating experience for children. Big open spaces with numerous things to explore and with other children running around to compete with can be just too much for many children. Here is a prime example from one mother:

> *As soon as the summer began, my daughter, Tina, began losing control of her bladder and urinating on herself and in the house. This behavior had cleared up since last summer, but now it was back. I was at my wits end – the stench of the urine was more than I could handle. Honestly, I wanted her out of my house – for good. I just didn't know how I was going to handle another summer like the ones previous. When I talked with my therapist, I mentioned that since the beginning of the summer, Tina was playing outside, all day long with her siblings and neighborhood friends. My therapist was able to make the connection between Tina's increase in stress level and the increased time of outdoor play. I began to understand that while playing outside is good for children, for Tina this kind of unregulated free play was far too much for her neurological system. Her body had become dysregulated and she was so hyper-aroused internally that she had lost control of her bodily signals.*
>
> *Consequencing or punishing Tina, or even talking to her about using the bathroom, was ineffective. What Tina needed was less time in a big open environment and more "check-in" time with me. As I began to regulate Tina's playtime and provide more opportunities for Tina to connect with me, Tina's system was able to settle back down and return to a state of regulation and balance. The urinating issue virtually disappeared within a week.*

The same is true for school environments. Too many children on the playground with too few adults is a threatening environment. Think about the last time you went onto a playground, whether at your child's school or at a local park. Where did the children gravitate to when you walked onto the playground? They came to you! Children naturally seek regulated adults when they are in overwhelming environments.

Some children may need you to limit the amount of space they play in or limit the amount of time they play together. When given the choice to either stay in the library or go to recess, many children who have had difficulties becoming aggressive during recess have actually chosen the library. They inherently know they do not feel safe in the playground.

Chart of Social Difficulties

Physical Difficulties:
1. Physical proximity
   a. Child keeps touching the other children and has no sense of personal space. Other children complain, "tell him to stop touching me."
   b. Child pushes other children out of the way to join the conversation.
   c. Child is "in your face" when talking.
2. Body Gestures
   a. The child's body language doesn't match the event. Example: the child waves too strongly in an exaggerated way when saying goodbye.
   b. The child's body movements don't seem to connect with what he is saying.
3. Eye Contact
   a. Child can't look others in the eye.
   b. Child stares to the point of being uncomfortable.

Verbal Difficulties:
1. Turn-taking
   a. Consistently interrupts.
   b. Doesn't allow time for someone else to have a turn talking.
   c. Insists on going first.
2. Timing
   a. Child talks too fast.
   b. Child shares way too much information to the point that the other person becomes irritated and bored.
   c. Child doesn't have an understanding of pause time – how long you need to wait before adding to the conversation.
   d. Child doesn't know how to add a comment or let others speak.

3. Voice
   a. Speaks too loudly or too softly, especially in relation to the distance of the other person (Example: child talks to you as if you're standing 10 feet away and you're only 1 foot away).
   b. Talks in a monotone.
   c. Speaks in a way that you can't understand him.
4. Feedback
   a. Child doesn't give any signals that he is listening to you.
   b. Child gives inappropriate and sometimes rude feedback, "You're fat."
5. Beginnings and endings
   a. Child jumps into a conversation with no transition or introducing himself.
   b. Child closes the conversation by simply walking away when he is done talking, with no goodbye.
   c. Child doesn't acknowledge others when they join the group.

Thinking Difficulties

1. Feelings
   a. Child is not attuned to the other person's feelings. ("Can I see where you buried your dog today?")
   b. Child does not consider how the impact of what he says may affect someone. (Child is given a new Spiderman toy for his birthday and says, "I hate Spiderman.")
   c. Child has little to no awareness of current situations. (You're in the middle of an upsetting conversation and your child asks you go buy food for his gerbil.)
2. Humor
   a. Laughs or talks at inappropriate times or situations.
b. Takes jokes and sarcasm literally.
c. Cannot distinguish between someone laughing "with " him or laughing "at" him.

Teachers can also limit the amount of space a child plays in to create safety. *"Jimmy, I want to make sure you feel safe when you're at recess today, so how about you just play right around here instead of the whole playground?"* Limiting this space and staying in close proximity can prevent a child from becoming scared and aggressive during recess.

At a school for emotionally challenged children, a fifth grade class with children ranging from ages 10 to 13 was on the playground. The teacher and the aid were in the middle of the playground sitting and talking on the picnic table. Instead of playing, the children continued to migrate around the picnic table. The teacher kept saying, *"Go on... scat...go play. Stop hanging around this table."*

These children were communicating their needs, yet the teacher was not "listening." What a perfect opportunity to teach these children how to interact. But all too often these opportunities are missed and we view children as "irritating," as in this example.

These children needed to have a regulated adult help them learn to interact and to keep the social environment safe, right there in their own environment (not in a therapy session talking about it later in the day). Here is what happened in this story:

The on-site therapist walked onto the playground. She checked in with the teacher to see if it would be alright if she interacted with the children during their recess. She organized a game of tag and played with the children. When disagreements arose and issues of fairness surfaced, she was there to help guide them and help them learn to stay regulated instead of becoming aggressive and defiant. For the first time ever, not one child in this class had to be disciplined, had points removed from his point chart, or was sent for a time-out during recess.

These children were able to play and interact appropriately because the element of fear and survival was eliminated. Children are able to get outside of their own perspective when they feel safe; it is then that the world no longer revolves around them. When they are secure, they have the capacity to connect. It comes down to one basic principle: Children cannot see another child's perspective until they get out of survival.

■

Children cannot see another child's perspective until they get out of survival.

■

The Traditional View neglects to understand or address this basic principle of human behavior. The ability to be socially connected does not come from a cognitive framework. Rather, the ability to be socially connected comes from non-cognitive capacities like empathy and synchrony. These are what connect us to other people.

This is best stated by Richard Davidson, director of the Laboratory for Affective Neuroscience at the University of Wisconsin: *"All emotions are social. You can't separate the cause of an emotion from the world of relationships – our social interactions are what drive our emotions."*[11]

Provide a child safety, unconditional love, and support to meet his emotional needs and you will be equipping him with the capacity to have effective and appropriate social skills for life.

Parenting Example: Social Skills

Scenario: Peter was turning 5 years old. His parents decided to invite some of the neighborhood children over to play and have a cupcake to celebrate Peter's birthday. When the children began arriving with their parents, Peter refused to go play with the children and instead wanted to be near the adults. As Peter's dad began socializing with the other parents, Peter started climbing onto the counter. Peter's dad reminded Peter that this behavior was against the house rules and encouraged Peter to go play with his friends. Peter became agitated, jumping around, and again began climbing on the counter.

Traditional View

Peter is clearly trying to ruin the conversation his father is having with the other parents and is just being disruptive. Peter needs to learn to respect adults and be polite and courteous when they are speaking to one another.

Additionally, Peter's parents have planned this party just for Peter and he needs to go play with the other children, not hang around the adults. It is so important for Peter to learn to socialize and begin developing friendships. Being that it is his birthday and he will be the center of attention, this should be the easiest day of the year to interact easily and appropriately with his playmates.

Peter's dad finally has enough of this behavior and takes Peter to the other room to play with the other children. Dad explains to Peter these children have come over to play with Peter and that he needs to stop being rude and needs to play with them. Dad reminds Peter that he knows how to be nice and that he needs to use his manners with the other children. Dad returns to the other room.

Within minutes, Peter is back in the room with his dad and the other adults. He continues to be disruptive so dad gives Peter the choice to either go play with the other children or go to his room for a time-out. This exchange escalates and dad, in his state of complete frustration and embarrassment, ultimately threatens Peter with no cupcake for being rude to him and to his friends.

A New View

Dad recognizes there is so much going on at their house that Peter is getting dysregulated and overwhelmed. Dad excuses himself from the adult conversation and takes Peter into the living room, away from everybody, to talk to him and help him calm down.

Dad gently holds Peter and puts him on his lap. Dad breathes and calms his own nervous system. Dad realizes that he was beginning to get embarrassed in front of the other parents with Peter's behavior so he acknowledges this feeling and gets himself focused on what is going on with Peter. Being mindful that his deep voice can be scary for Peter, Dad softens his tone and lowers the volume of his voice when speaking to Peter. Dad begins asking a few questions to see if he can work to understand what has Peter so upset.

After a few dead end questions, Peter finally blurts out, "Cupcake!" and immediately relaxes into his dad's arms. Dad realizes what the fear is for Peter – he is worried that he will not get a cupcake! Peter sees all the adults and children and he is afraid there would not be enough cupcakes. He is afraid he would not get his cupcake on his special day. Dad reassures Peter that he will definitely get his cupcake and takes Peter by the hand. He has Peter point out the cupcake he wants. Dad picks up the cupcake and places it in a special place and reassures him that nobody is allowed this cupcake except Peter.

Peter smiles and he runs off to play. His fear is calmed and he now has the capacity to play nicely with his friends. Dad reflects about how important this interaction was for the two of them. Dad realizes if he had implemented traditional parenting techniques and threatened to not give Peter a cupcake because of his disruptive behavior, Dad would have only been creating more fear in a child who was acting out because of fear. Dad also realizes the opportunity for Peter to play and to be the birthday boy with his friends is a valuable and memorable experience for Peter that was not lost.

True story!

Quick Reference
Social Skills

Remember that a child struggling socially:
- May be a reminder of the parent's social challenges from their own childhood.
- Is being driven from a state of fear...it is not a conscious choice.
- Is hyper-aroused and will have a difficult time connecting at the cognitive and rational level.
- Needs a regulated adult to attend to his emotional needs.
- Will learn social skills through experiencing it with a regulated, safe, and nurturing adult.
- Is likely much younger emotionally and developmentally than his peers.

When helping a child struggling socially, recognize that he needs you to:
- Align with your own fears of him not having friends for the rest of his life.
- Give him understanding rather than lecturing him.
- Be a "safe base" for him so he can regulate through his relationship with you.
- Be proactive and interrupt or shorten his play time so he does not get too overwhelmed.
- Provide a smaller area to play instead of a large open play space.
- Provide calmer social environments to avoid becoming overwhelmed in the beginning (Chuck E. Cheese may be too much!).
- Model loving and safe social interactions so he can experience this beyond his cognitive thinking level.
- Connect with him so he can express and work through his fears with you.

CHAPTER EIGHT

Demanding

■

"Have a vision. Be demanding."

– Colin Powell

Demanding, strong-willed, determined, dominant, resistant, stubborn – these are all typical descriptors of a child who is difficult to be around and difficult to parent. Historically, the demanding child has also been seen as the "spoiled" child, or worse, a "spoiled brat."

When children act demanding, the stigma of having a spoiled child can be a difficult barrier for parents. There is a tremendous amount of judgment placed not only on a demanding child (hence the term spoiled brat) but on the parents, as well. Socially, a demanding child has been seen as a direct result of parents being too permissive or too lenient.

Demanding children often bring out the worst in their parents. When faced with the social stigma of having a bratty child in addition to being faced continually with a child who will not respond to his parents can drive the parent well past the parent's own window of stress tolerance. Parents often hit their breaking point and, in desperation, begin yelling and reacting to their children in ways they promised themselves they would never do. Ironically, the result is that parents model exactly the same type of behavior they are trying to change.

Carlos is a demanding child who is difficult to satisfy and please. He constantly wants his own way, always wanting the opposite of what his parents are asking. Most of his demanding and oppositional behaviors are seen at home, not at school, with friends, or with his grandparents. In fact, his teachers have a difficult time believing his parents when they describe the blow-outs and power struggles that happen at home. He is for the most part a well-mannered, agreeable child at school. Yet at home, when Carlos doesn't get his way with his parents, he will become so demanding that he will eventually start throwing and breaking things, yelling, and even urinating on the carpet to get his way with his parents.

Traditional View

Traditional parenting advice for demanding children has worked on the premise of determining the difference between what a child "wants" and what a child "needs" to extinguish the demanding behavior from the child. A recent pediatric advisory from the University of Michigan states that some parents "confuse the child's needs (for example, feeding) with his wishes (for example, for play)." [1] This advisory explicitly states that children have tantrums "to get your attention, to wear you down, to get you to change your mind, and to get their own way."[2] Parents are told to ignore these tantrums and to never give in to their children.

Maintaining control through strict boundaries is emphasized in traditional literature for parenting demanding children. Parents are told they can shift their child's behavior by getting their child to "desire" compliance by removing liberties and privileges.[3] Parents are reminded their demanding children are willfully defying them and that much of what they do is just to get noticed.

Traditional articles and books describing a demanding child warn that much of what children do is simply for attention. The word "undue attention" is often used and some literature states that children as young as 5 or 6 months of age have the ability to cry and fuss deliberately to get their own way.[4] Giving in to this attention-seeking behavior is said to be detrimental and will only spoil the child.

Punishment is also seen as a necessity for demanding and defiant children. The well-known family expert, Dr. James Dobson, recommends spanking children: "Many children desperately need this resolution to their disobedience"[5] He further states, "An appropriate spanking is the shortest and most effective route to an attitude adjustment...justice must speak swiftly and eloquently."[6] According to such advice, the solution for the case with Carlos above would be to spank him immediately. Carlos has exhibited stiff-necked rebellion and the parent had better take it out of him. Pain is an excellent purifier.[7]

A New View

It is interesting that the Traditional View works very hard to make a distinction between children having a "need" versus children having a "want." In the New View, however, the most basic question has to be, "Is there really a difference?" All negative behavior arises from a place of stress (see chapter one, *"Beyond Consequences, Logic, & Control,* Volume 1), so how can one distinguish between the two? They are one and the same.

Children act out because they need attention, not because they want it. It is a cry for attachment and nurturing, not willful disobedience. Negative behavior is a communication of a need to feel safe, secure, validated, loved, approved, acknowledged, and wanted. If we were to follow the advice outlined in the traditional model, such as ignoring the child or, worse, spanking the child, these deep intrinsic needs not only would be disregarded but would be exasperated and increased. The message being sent to the child would be, *"Your needs are not important to me"* and *"Don't turn to me for support and love; you'll have to find that on your own."* This serves only to leave children in a place of aloneness, anger, fear, and overwhelm.

> ■
>
> *Negative behavior is a communication of a need to feel safe, secure, validated, loved, approved, acknowledged, and wanted.*
>
> ■

An adult parented as a child under the premises of the Traditional View writes, *"My relationship with my parents may never be repaired. They do not understand the humiliation and frustration and anger they created within me when they struck me."* Parenting from the standpoint of seeing the behavior as the sole focus leaves no room for consideration of the relationship between the parent and child. The relationship becomes strained and the child is left with nowhere safe to turn. The person with whom they are biologically designed to turn to for help, protection, love, and security is now the source of pain, conflict, and fear.

When the child's underlying desire for love, acceptance, and validation is ignored and disregarded, a child will learn to move away emotionally from the parent instead of moving to connect with the parent. Attachment research demonstrates that the impact of the parent-child attachment directly influences the child's ability to comply with his parents. A study published in *School Psychology International* suggests "secure attachment to parents is negatively associated with conduct problems." In other words, the stronger the relationship between the child and parent, the fewer the behavioral problems. The study also states "consistent responsiveness to the child's emotional needs by the caregiver helps build a positive working model

> ■
>
> *In other words, the stronger the relationship between the child and parent, the fewer the behavioral problems.*
>
> ■

of the world and those in it as approachable and safe."[9] Meeting children through emotional awareness and emotional attunement gives them the feeling of knowing they are safe and the world around them is safe.

Children inherently need to have connection with their parents to be able to learn to regulate their emotional states. It is a biological and physiological need. We are designed to be in relationship with one another. When a child is feeling insecure, he will naturally seek the connection and relationship with his parent. Yet for some children, depending on their innate personalities and negative early childhood experiences, the only way they know how to seek this connection is through demanding behaviors. This is the only way they know how to communicate their internal quest for connection. For many adopted and foster children, this is what was previously modeled for them from their former caretakers. They are only repeating that which was taught to them.

We need to respond to this demanding behavior with the interpretation that it is simply relationship-seeking behavior. A parent's response needs to be a positive and loving response, not an isolating, damaging reaction. The parent needs to realize a demanding child is simply a scared child. It is the child's way of saying, *"I need to know I'm alright and I need to know that you'll pay enough attention to me so I know I'm safe and that you are here for me."*

Interpreting this child's need for connection as "willful disobedience," as described through the lens of the Traditional View, assumes the child is fully cognitive and rational in his stress state. When in a calm state of arousal, most children know how to ask politely for attention or connection. Yet, when children are stressed out and beyond their window of stress tolerance (and for some children, this is 90 percent to 100 percent of the time), they easily shift into a state of overwhelm and revert to negative, demanding behaviors.

For children with traumatic histories, the operating program in their minds tells them they are unsafe. Accessing their cognitive, rational, thinking brain (their neocortex) is not possible. Research tells us that stress causes an impairment in our ability to think clearly during times of heightened stress. Stress also causes us to react in exaggerated ways. Think about the last time you were overly stressed. Your perception of a situation was more than likely much worse than it was in reality or your thought process convinced you that you were much less equipped or weaker than you were.

This same dynamic happens with our children. An intense response of demanding the parent see it his way *("If you don't agree with me, I will die.")* is an example of a child's need to feel safe. Giving in or backing down for this child is literally a death sentence. As the beginning quote suggests, when you have a vision, be demanding. The vision for children with an intense level of demanding behaviors is life over death. Put yourself in this position: if you lived in a state of survival, you would be the most demanding person on this planet.

A demanding child is a child who needs to feel heard, understood, and safe. Any time we seek to control someone or a situation, it is because we ourselves are feeling out of control. In the example with Carlos, giving the "control" back to him through connecting with him in relationship by listening, offering understanding, acknowledgement, and validation is the key to de-escalating this type of behavior and helping him learn to regulate such strong emotions. The dialogue might look something like this:

> ■
>
> *Anytime we seek to control someone or a situation, it is because we ourselves are feeling out of control.*
>
> ■

Mom: *"Good morning, honey! It's time for breakfast, but I have to let you know we're out of Cheerios. So to make up for it, I made you some special pancakes."*

Carlos: *"What! No Cheerios! I hate you! I want Cheerios!"*

Mom: *"I know you were expecting Cheerios, sweetheart; and it is so hard to expect something and then not get it."*

Carlos: *"I don't want your stupid pancakes. I want my Cheerios."*

Mom: *"This is really hard, isn't it?"*

Carlos: *"Why don't you have my Cheerios? You know I like my Cheerios. I have to have my Cheerios. Go to the store and get me my Cheerios!!!!"*

Mom: *"It probably feels like I don't love you when I don't get you exactly what you want, doesn't it?"*

Carlos: *"Go buy them right now!"*

Mom: *"I love you and I'm sorry we are out of your favorite breakfast."*

Carlos: *"You don't love me. If you did, you would go to the store right now and buy them for me!"*

Mom: *"This is so disappointing for you and I'm sure it feels like I don't love you right now."*

Carlos: *"Go to hell!"*

Mom: (breathing and staying out of her child's fear state) *"I'm right here with you always, honey. I'm not leaving you. I love you."*

Carlos: (beginning to shift from a state of hyper-arousal to a state of calm) *"Ummmhhh!"*

Mom: (Mom works to stay present, offers her loving silence, and allows Carlos the emotional space to make a shift back to regulation and safety.)

Carlos: (after a long stint of silence) *"I hate my life!*

Mom: *"Really? What's going on, honey?"*

Carlos: *"Nothing is ever the way it is supposed to be. I'm supposed to be at football practice today but I didn't make the cut! I was supposed to be invited to a party last weekend but my friends left me out. I'm supposed to be doing better in my math class but I failed the test even after studying. Now I'm supposed to be eating Cheerios and you don't even have any!"*

Mom: *"May I give you a hug?"*

Carlos: (nods his head)

Mom: (gives Carlos a hug) *"I'm sorry life is so hard for you right now. I love you."*

In this dialogue, Mom was able to create safety and security despite Carlos' intensified state of fear. The beginning description of Carlos in this chapter stated his demanding behaviors would eventually escalate into throwing and breaking objects. This was prevented by the responses his mom was able to give to him. She did not focus on his disrespect, his foul language, or his demanding behavior for the moment. Mom was able to stay regulated enough to keep focused on the core issue of Carlos not feeling alright with his life. It was not about the Cheerios and it was not a personal attack against her.

While it may seem minor to us as adults to not have a bowl of Cheerios, to a child with a traumatic history, most of which includes abandonment, neglect, and/or abuse, such an event is interpreted as, *"You don't love me and you are going to leave me just like everybody else in my life!"* This child's programming only knows this reaction. A child whose history includes a major attachment break lives in a constant state of fear that he will be hurt again, abandoned again, and/or rejected again. It is the parent's responsibility to understand this child's framework and for the child to have a new experience. This mom was able to refrain from taking Carlos' reactions

■

You cannot override fear with more fear.

■

personally. Any time we take something personally, we automatically feel attacked and become defensive. This reactionary stance serves only to add more fear into such a dialogue. You cannot override fear with more fear.

While on the surface it looks as if Carlos is attacking his mother verbally, and certainly if you were the mom in this example, it would feel like you were being attacked (especially since mom made the extra effort to substitute special pancakes for the Cheerios.) However, it takes going beyond the behaviors. It takes parenting at a higher level of consciousness and living life at a higher level of awareness to see through the layers of anger, disrespect, and the demanding behaviors. If you have difficulty being reactive, say to yourself, *"It's not about me."*

Just as Superman has x-ray vision, parents can develop their x-ray vision into the heart and soul of their children. That is the place of connection and relationship. When a parent can reach into this place of internal turmoil, healing at all levels is possible for the child. Through her x-ray vision in this example with Carlos, the mom in the example was able to:

- Understand Carlos' reaction and relate to his experiences of rejection, abandonment, and pain
- Reach Carlos at his emotional core
- Soothe his stress state
- Pour unconditional love into a soul that was vacant of such love
- Give Carlos emotional space to be angry
- Acknowledge and validate his disappointment
- Stay focused on her relationship with Carlos
- Stay confident that Carlos' demands were only demands for safety and security
- Put aside her own fears of having a bratty or unruly child
- Work on her own regulation in order not to drive Carlos into a deeper state of fear

But you're saying, *"What about the way he was treating his mother? This is unacceptable behavior!"* Remember that at the moment of dysregulation and escalated behaviors, it simply cannot be about the behavior, and the child is unable to learn appropriate behaviors. The behaviors are only a symptom of the core issue. When we address the behaviors at such a moment, it is then we typically see not less of this type of behavior, but more of it. You cannot demand a child stop being so demanding and expect results. It is the parent's responsibility to read these behaviors in the moment, respond to them, dance with them, and create an environment of safety, love, and validation.

> ■
>
> *You cannot demand that a child stop being so demanding and expect results.*
>
> ■

The teaching and learning of appropriate behaviors and manners comes afterwards. Once Carlos is calm, the parent can then talk with Carlos about how he can express himself in a more respectful way. The parent can take this opportunity to express how his behavior makes her feel. This helps teach empathy and helps Carlos realize his actions directly affect others. The parent can ask Carlos how he could do it differently next time, giving him a voice and giving him a sense of control. They can make it fun by doing some roleplays, each reversing the other's role.

When we stay focused on why our children are acting out and being demanding, it keeps us in a place of love and acceptance. Children who display demanding behaviors are needing attention. Seeing this behavior through the lens of willful disobedience or perceiving the child is being a brat will only move the parent further from being able to address the child's cry for relationship. The child's vision is connection, relationship, and security. Embrace this vision and accept their demand for it, knowing you will have the opportunity to teach him more respectful ways to do it in the future.

> ■
>
> *Seeing this behavior through the lens of willful disobedience or perceiving that the child is being a brat, will only move the parent further from being able to address the child's cry for relationship.*
>
> ■

Parenting Example: Demanding Behavior

Scenario: Mom and her two sons are running late for school this morning, as is the case most mornings. They are running late today because neither of the two boys (Nick – age 6, and Joshua–age 9) had responded to mom's request to brush their teeth, get their backpacks, or put on their shoes. So mom is exhausted and stressed because she has already helped them do these tasks. She then asks them to get into the car and put on their seatbelts while she locks up the house and puts their backpacks in the car. Nick waits until she gets into the car and buckles her seatbelt and begins demanding that mom put his seatbelt on for him.

Traditional View

Nick: *"No. You put my seatbelt on."*

Mom: (with an exasperated tone). *"You know how to put your seatbelt on Nick. I'd like you to do it please."*

Nick: *"No, I want you to do it."*

Mom: *"You can do it. You're 6 years old. You've been doing it yourself for six months or more now."*

Nick: *"No, I want you to do it."*

Mom: (really exasperated and starting to get angry) *"You've already made us late by not listening to me in the house and now you've waited until I'm already in the car and have my seatbelt on and then you demand that I do your seatbelt. Well, I'm not going to do it. You need to do it yourself."*

Nick: *"No. I won't. You can't make me."* (Nick stands up and refuses to sit down.)

Mom: *"Nick, we are late for school, thanks to you. You need to sit down and put your seat belt on now."*

Nick: (screaming) *"NO!"* (He picks up a full water bottle from the back seat and throws it across the car into the front. Then he picks up a library book and throws it at the windshield.)

Mom: (really angry now and yelling). *"NICK! You can't throw things in the car like that. Someone will get hurt."*

Mom gets out of the car and tries with force to put Nick in his seat. Nick kicks and punches mom. Eventually mom gets the seat belt on but everyone is completely dysregulated and the tension is thick and uncomfortable. The trip to school is horrible and they arrive 15 minutes late for school.

A New View

Before getting in the car, Mom realizes she is tired and dysregulated because of everything that has transpired this morning. She takes a few minutes to just stop. She takes some deep breaths and acknowledges how she is feeling. She gets in the car and puts on her seatbelt, staying mindful to be present with her boys, knowing her number one responsibility in the mornings is to send her children off to school as regulated as possible.

Mom: *"Gee, that was a difficult morning, wasn't it boys? I'm feeling a bit dysregulated."*

Joshua: *"Ding, ding, ding."* (This is Joshua imitating the sound of a bell, signalling they all need to take three deep breaths to help calm themselves. Joshua and Mom take three deep breaths.)

Nick: (Speaking in an angry and defiant tone). *"I'm not breathing and I'm not putting my seatbelt on. I want you to do it."*

Mom: (Speaking in a gentle and kind tone). *"Of course, sweetheart. I can do that for you."*

Mom: (Mom gets out and goes to put the seatbelt on for him. Nick grabs Mom's hair and pulls it.) *"Oww, that hurts, Nick. I can see you're not feeling safe right now. I know it is sometimes hard for you to leave the house and get in the car."*

Nick: (Still pulling on the hair) *"No, it's not!"*

Mom: *"I know going to school is sometimes scary for you."*

Nick: *"I want you to stay with me at school."*

Mom: *"Sure, darling. I can stay at school with you for as long as you want me to. I will always look after you and keep you safe."* (Mom had previously made arrangements with her boss to have flexibility on her arrival time to work for situations just like this).

Nick: (Nick lets go of Mom's hair and lets her put his seatbelt on. Mom gives Nick a big hug and a kiss.)

Mom: *"I love you, Nick."*

Nick: *"I love you, Mom."*

Joshua: *"What about me?"*

Mom: *"I love you, too, Joshua, very much. And thanks for ringing the bell and helping me calm down earlier."*

Mom goes around to Joshua's side of the car and gives him a big hug and a kiss. They leave for school, everyone is regulated, and they are all feeling better. They arrive at school only five minutes late and when mom asks Nick if he needs her to stay at school for awhile, Nick replies, "Nah, I'm okay, Mom."

After school, Mom reconnects with Nick and discusses the events of the morning. Nick is open to listening to Mom's suggestions. Mom expresses to Nick how painful it was when he grabbed her hair, not in a shaming way, but in a loving way to help Nick learn empathy. Nick apologizes on his own and commits to making changes in his behavior in the future.

True story!

Quick Reference
Demanding

Remember that a demanding child:
- Is expressing his needs in the only way he knows how, for the moment.
- Has a much deeper underlying issue far beyond the behavior.
- Is seeking connection from you, not punishment or a lecture.
- Needs a strong parent-child relationship to reduce his negative behaviors.
- Feels if he backs down or gives in, he may die.
- Is being demanding because he has a need to be heard and understood.
- Needs you to stop demanding that he stop demanding.

When helping a demanding child, recognize he needs you to:
- Ignore the behavior but not ignore his needs underlying the demanding behavior.
- Open up the space for him to be able to express what is really stressing him out.
- Be safe so he can feel safe enough to drop the demanding behaviors.
- Work to understand and relate to his pain.
- Stay focused on the relationship, not the words.
- Remember that his demands are simply demands for safety and love.
- Put aside your own fears of how the world is going to judge you as a weak parent.
- Work on your own regulation to keep from being pulled into his stress vortex.
- Teach him better ways to express himself once he calms down.

CHAPTER NINE

Self Injury

∎

"The body says what words cannot."
– Martha Graham

"I draw my razor slowly across the flesh, feeling it bite deep into the meat of my arm. For a second, a white, gaping gash is visible, with some yellowish fat around it. Then its cavern is filled with rich, red-black blood. It runs down my arm, trickling over the white lines of older scars and the thick pink keloids of the newer ones."

These are the words of a 16-year-old "cutter." Graphic and un-nerving, but a true reality for some children (and adults). Self-injury, also termed self-mutilation, self-destructive behavior, and self-harming behavior, can be a response to traumatic childhood experiences.[1] The most powerful predictor of self-destructive behavior is neglect.

Van der Kolk, Perry, and Herman found that while childhood trauma can contribute to the start of this type of behavior, the continuation of such behavior is due to a lack of secure attachment to a parent or caregiver. Their research showed those "who could not remember feeling special or loved by anyone as children were least able to control their self-destructive behavior."[2]

Self-injurious behaviors can also include the following: head-banging, carving, scratching, branding, marking, burning, biting, bruising, hitting, picking, and pulling at skin and hair. The forms and severity of self-injury can vary, but all are indicators of a child who is feeling terrified, dysregulated, and internally explosive.

Self-mutilation can be extremely challenging for parents and care-takers, as well as for professionals. Can you imagine taking a razor blade to your arm, as described above, and then feeling relief and feeling as if you are "grounded" and "whole"? How can watching, with intent and focus, your blood flowing from a purposeful, planned cut you have just created feel good? For the majority of us, this is a concept well beyond comprehension.

Yet, we must remember children generally do things for reasons that make sense to them.

Jaynee's mom noticed her arm one day and absolutely "freaked out," as Jaynee put it. Her mom was aghast at the cuts on her daughter's arm. Jaynee had been clever enough to hide the marks over the past few months, but on this day, Jaynee let her guard down and pulled up her sleeves when she got warm. Her mother was walking by and before Jaynee could pull down her sleeves to cover up the remnants of the previous month's cuts, her mother became reactive and explosive.

■

We must remember that children generally do things for reasons that make sense to them.

■

"What are you doing to yourself? When did you start cutting on your arms? What is going on with you? What were you thinking?"

Jaynee knew her mother wasn't open to understanding how the cutting was actually helping her feel better. Yet that is how it made Jaynee feel. When Jaynee cut, she felt a sense of peace and relief. If Jaynee could describe it to someone, the one word she would choose would be "happy." So, the next night when Jaynee felt the urge to cut, she started cutting the underside of her feet, keeping her habit safe from her mother.

Traditional View

Traditionally, self-injury has been seen as so severe that a child who self-injures needs to be seen by a mental health professional. Few parenting books discuss this topic. Parenting experts have left this behavior to trained professionals.

The traditional approach for many professionals has been to give the child a diagnosis to explain this type of behavior. The most common diagnosis assigned to a child who self-injures is borderline personality disorder (BPD). Other common diagnoses are depression and dysthymia. In many cases, it is not unusual for a child to have two of these, or even all three, of these diagnoses.

Treatment for self-injurious behaviors traditionally works from a cognitive-behavioral framework. The "Stages of Change," developed to help smokers quit their habit or addiction, is often used to help patients "begin thinking about change as well as the benefits and barriers to change." [3] Questions at the cognitive level of thought are used, such as "Who is in control of your life – the cutting or you?" This approach works to point out the distasteful aspects of cutting, such as the scarring, secrecy, shame, infections, and stigma, to help the patient make better choices.

"Therapeutic approaches involving cognitive restructuring, behavioral modifications, motivational interviewing, assertiveness training, and teaching alternative coping mechanisms are the common practice in working with self-injurious behaviors."[4] Activities such as journaling and using "Self-injury Logs" or "Impulse Control Logs" are assigned to patients. All of these approaches and activities are used with the goal of empowering self-injurers to make healthier choices. Inpatient hospital programs are also an option. These programs run for 30 days and the cost is about $20,000 with admission of children as young as 12 years old.

When these approaches are ineffective, medication is considered as the next course of action. Anti-depressants, mood stabilizers, and antipsychotic medications are suggested by professionals.[5]

A New View

It is important to note that traditional parenting resources that discuss other severe childhood behaviors only minimally discuss the topic of self-injury and many do not mention self-injury in their spectrum of behaviors. If the resource does include self-injury, the depth to which it develops this behavior is shallow and vague. It is as if the authors are saying, "Well, I need to at least mention it, but I don't know what to do about it, so I'll move onto the next behavior."

Resources that take a strong stance on parenting issues such as demanding children make eye contact or adamantly making the point that parents must take control of their children, yet dance and float around this issue of self-mutilation, need to be questioned. What is the nature of this discrepancy? Perhaps we need to take a closer look at the professionals developing these parenting techniques. Skirting the topic of self-injurious behavior is a direct reflection of one's inability to handle the depth of pain and anguish children with this behavior experience. To comprehend such behavior, it truly takes understanding and allowing one's self to identify with this level of pain. It takes opening up to experiencing this level of discomfort within one's own mind and heart.

Traditional techniques are often focused on stopping the self-injurious behavior as quickly as possible. Shutting down this behavior is a reflection of how uncomfortable professionals and parents are with this behavior. It repulses them, makes them feel ineffective, and frightens them. For professionals, this behavior threatens them clinically. *"If this child goes too far and accidentally kills herself, I will be investigated by my board. My license is at risk."* With such fear intertwined within the therapeutic process, a useful and meaningful therapeutic relationship cannot be formed, blocking the road to healing for the child.

Self-mutilating behavior is often seen to be resistant to therapeutic intervention by professionals working within the traditional framework. More often than not, this is not a reflection of the child's resistance to change but rather the professional's resistance to exploring this type of behavior with the child at the level at which it needs to be explored. If a therapist, either consciously or subconsciously, is fearful of this type of behavior, this will only impede the child's ability to make significant changes. Blaming the ineffectiveness of therapy on the intervention neglects to consider the emotional openness of the professional implementing the intervention. So we must ask ourselves, if an adult has difficulty handling this level of emotional stress, how can we expect our children to handle it appropriately? The reality is that our level of comfort will directly impact a child's ability to work through her own fear and stress to shift out of self-mutilating behaviors.

■

The reality is that our level of comfort will directly impact a child's ability to work through her own fear and stress in order to shift out of self-mutilating behaviors.

■

Additionally, when a child's self-injurious behavior does not improve, perhaps it isn't that this behavior is resistant to therapeutic intervention but rather the therapeutic intervention is missing the key element to healing: the relationship between the parent and child. Unfortunately, what typically happens in traditional approaches is that the parent is left in the waiting room, participating only as a bystander to the therapeutic process. If we recall the research noted at the beginning of this chapter, it clearly stated the continuation of this behavior is due to a lack of a secure attachment with the caregiver.

Reflecting on the example of Jaynee, where do these children do their cutting? They do it right in their own homes, not in the therapist's office. Such behaviors are emotionally driven. All the cognitive planning that may have occurred in the therapist's office the day before on how not to do this behavior will have little or no effect on the urgency to self-injure and to carry out this behavior. It is at that moment the child needs to have a safe place to turn for help. Relying on a cognitive behavioral plan is unreasonable. Here are a few quotes revealing the internal mindset of those who self-injure:

> *"Because I feel so much internal pain, I need a way to release it all. So by cutting myself, it acts as an outlet for the internal pain, like it's all running out of me, like water out of a tap."*

> *"I cut until I can get the pain to stop."*

> *"I feel like a pressure cooker that's going to explode. Cutting and bleeding sufficiently is like letting out the steam. If I do this to my satisfaction, I feel immediate relief, as if injected with valium or something. It helps stop the inner turmoil for a while. It becomes an addiction."*

> *"I'd rather have the physical pain instead of the emotional pain."*

> *"I am full of anger and hurt. I feel like nobody cares. I do it because it is easier for me to hurt myself and deal with my pain than it is to tell someone and hurt their feelings. I keep everything to myself and then it builds up. I explode and then start cutting."*

> *"I stopped because of the support I received."*

The thread running through these quotes is that the self-injurers have so much internal stress, yet have no one to turn to for release. Any of us, when faced with more internal stress than we can handle, will find external ways to cope if we feel we cannot talk to someone who can handle our stress and our pain. Some of us stuff ourselves with chocolate, others go shopping and justify buying another pair of shoes, some smoke, others drink, and the list goes on and on. These are all external attempts at soothing an uncomfortable, quite often intolerable, internal state. When we don't have someone to whom we can express ourselves, we seek these external means simply in an attempt to calm ourselves and escape the pain. They provide an escape from the anxiety, memories, and overwhelm.

Physiological Payoffs to Cutting. At a physiologic level, our bodies increase the production of cortisol when we become stressed. Cortisol is a hormone produced in the adrenal gland in response to stress. Thus, the level of cortisol excretion is an excellent way to measure one's stress level. A case study by Sachsse and other researchers showed self-injurious behaviors can actually reduce the cortisol level within the body. They traced the nightly cortisol levels in a woman with self-harming behaviors. On the days she cut, her cortisol levels were significantly lower than on the days she did not cut. [6] There is a physiological payoff for this type of behavior.

This study demonstrates why self-injury is often used by children with severe trauma histories. It provides an immediate, dramatic way to calm the body. The internal tension is immediately decreased. It is essentially an addictive behavior – an external attempt at soothing an internal state. Once they experience relief from this behavior – yet have not addressed the core of the emotional stress and pain underneath – the need to cut again will soon present itself. It becomes repetitive. Just like the chain smoker who experiences an immediate sense of relief with the first cigarette will have the urge to find the next cigarette soon after to maintain this level of internal payoff.

Additionally, self-injurious behaviors can create another dynamic. It can allow one to alter his level of consciousness. In his book, *The Boy Who Was Raised as a Dog,* Dr. Bruce Perry discusses how cutting can also induce a dissociative state. A dissociative state is a state that allows the mind to separate or compartmentalize certain memories or thoughts from normal consciousness. It is a way to avoid certain memories and thoughts too painful to keep in one's conscious awareness. It is an altered state of consciousness that allows one to escape from pain and stress, feeling little emotional or physical pain. Dr. Perry explains, "such experiences are linked with the release of high levels of opioids, the brain's natural heroin-like substances that kill pain and produce a calming sense of distance from one's troubles." [7]

Become a Safe Place. A quote from one cutter reads, "My only escape is blood." If a child feels his only escape is blood, we must look at the relationship between the parent and child. Children need a secure base to turn to when they are overwhelmed. The definition of "children" in this statement does not exclude any age group. Do we, as adults, sometimes feel the urgency to call our parents on the phone (even if deceased or emotionally estranged) when life becomes too much? It is biologically engrained in us.

When children do not feel they have this safe base with their parent(s), they will find other ways to regulate that can be dangerous. The child who wrote the statement, "My only escape is blood" was clearly without this secure base with his parent(s). As a parent, it becomes your responsibility to become this safe place for your child. If you are stressed out, you will in turn cause more stress for your child. While just the idea of seeing your child cutting herself is disturbing, it is your responsibility as a parent to own your reactions and take ownership of them. No matter the intensity of the situation, it is always your responsibility to process your reactions and fear as opposed to projecting them onto your child. All too often, this becomes the case during intense moments between parents and their children, which only hinders the healing process.

Healing happens when the parent can continue to reach out with unconditional love, acceptance, and tolerance to stay in a safe and supporting relationship with the child. Victimhood and blame need to be absent from the equation and be replaced by an openness to the other's own internal chaos. In doing so, fear will be replaced by love.

It takes believing and comprehending this important fact: "Children communicate through their behaviors." The parent's responsibility is to listen to this behavior, not to give a consequence for this behavior. Giving a consequence for the behavior is analogous to saying, *"Hush-up. I don't want to hear what you're saying. I'm the parent and you need to do as I say."* For a child who is cutting, this only sends her to do more cutting, feeling as if there is no other outlet, no other escape.

In reality, your child is saying, *"I feel completely helpless and I don't know what else to do. I feel like I'm hitting maximum capacity internally and I have to create this release valve or I might completely implode."* Helping your child release this pain comes through your relationship with her. Invite your child to come to you, *"Come here, sweetheart. I need to know how badly you hurt. Tell me what's so bad in your life."*

■

Helping your child to release this pain comes through your relationship with her.

■

It takes spending time with your child every day. If it feels like your child is a stranger in your home, it takes building this relationship through loving influence and a promise to be able to handle the extent of your child's pain. Create the dynamic of communication. Open the air for emotional expression. Trust that you have the ability to help your child unlike anyone else in the world. Explore with your child why she is cutting:

"I know that sometimes you hurt so badly inside that you hurt

yourself on the outside. I'd like to understand this. People do it for so many reasons; if you could help me understand why you do it, I'd be grateful." If your child cannot express why she cuts, you can make suggestions such as, *"I think it is when you get so stressed and your pain becomes unbearable that you want to cut."*

Interrupt the Negative Cycle. Offer a new solution:

"When you feel this way, I want you to come to me. It doesn't matter what time of the day, I want you to come get me so you don't have to hurt yourself any longer. I won't freak out like I have in the past. I'm here to support you and love you in a way I haven't been able to do in the past. I don't want you alone in this."

Be available. If your child comes to you, stop everything you're doing to connect with her. Realize it has taken all the courage inside her to make this initiation to connect with you. Work through some of the following questions with your child to create more understanding for the both of you:

1. "Why do I feel like I need to hurt myself? What has happened in my life that brought me to this point?"
2. "When was the first time I cut? What happened that led to this initial event?"
3. "How does it feel when I cut myself?"
4. "What will it take for me to come to my parent/grandparent/caretaker the next time I get the urge?"

Provide alternatives that are relationally based. Suggest going for a walk, going out for a drive, renting a movie, or reading the comics together. Bringing something pleasant into an unpleasant situation can be refreshing. You are not avoiding the issue, just adding a level of comfort to it and breaking the negative feedback loop through your relationship with your child.

Avoid any type of punitive action. Punishment and guilt simply feed the cycle of self-harm and your child will become more mindful to hide it and to cover up her actions. Relating back to the example at the beginning of this

> ■
>
> *Negative reactions only perpetuate the self-injurious cycle at an underground level.*
>
> ■

chapter, Jaynee didn't stop cutting, she only became more savvy at it when her mother reacted to this behavior. Negative reactions only perpetuate the self-injurious cycle at an underground level.

Your goal as a parent is help your child see there is another way out. Keep this at the forefront of your mind when interacting with your child. There is an alternative to escape from the pain, and that escape is through you. You have the ability to help your child simply through putting love into action. Recall the research cited earlier, stating the continuation of this behavior comes from a lack of attachment and a lack of feeling special and truly loved. Creating the healing environment your child needs comes first through the ownership of your own reactions and then through acceptance, tolerance, patience, openness, persistence, and a deep level of trusting in the power of love.

Parenting Example: Self-Injury

Scenario: Mom knocks on her 14-year-old adopted daughter's bedroom door and without waiting for a response mom opens the door. Her daughter, Erin, quickly puts her hands behind her back. Mom asks her what she is hiding and Erin quickly responds, "Nothing!" Mom continues to ask and finally demands that Erin show her. Erin shows her a calligraphy pen and after mom's questioning, Erin tells her she has been using it to cut herself. Mom was shocked as she had never seen signs of this behavior and to make matters worse, she was the one who bought Erin the calligraphy pen.

Traditional View

Mom demands that Erin give back the pen. Erin begs to keep the pen, promising to never use the pen to cut again if mom would just let her keep it. Of course there was no way mom was going to let her daughter keep it, so mom quickly instituted a new policy. Erin was not to be in her room with her door closed at all. Erin became outraged, yelling back at her mother. For the next three days, Mom held this boundary until she was able to contact their therapist. Mom explained to the therapist that they had not spoken to each other in the past three days since this incident and that she was terrified that Erin would hurt herself. An emergency appointment was made for Erin to meet with the therapist to develop a treatment plan that included Erin keeping an impulse control log and filling out a worksheet with questions to help Erin make better choices.

After three months of working with the therapist, Mom discovered that Erin was continuing to cut. Mom was fortunate to find an inpatient unit that had an immediate opening. Erin was admitted to the 30-day program for treatment of her self-injurious behaviors. The program cost was $20,000. When Erin was in treatment, Mom was spending her time working with the insurance company to have them cover part of the expense of this program.

A New View

Mom stops and realizes her fear and anxiety over this issue is making this situation worse. Mom tells Erin she is upset at this moment and needs a timeout to calm herself down. She reassures Erin she'll be back in a little bit so they can talk this through without making it worse. Mom goes to her room, processes her fear, breathes, and works to change her perspective to that of her daughter's. She remembers this type of behavior is similar to the concept of taking a smoker's cigarettes away and expecting him to be able to stop. She knows even if she keeps the calligraphy pen, her daughter will find some way to continue this behavior. Mom waits until she is feeling calm enough to talk to Erin in an empathetic and calm manner.

Mom goes back to Erin's room and knocks on the door. Mom asks Erin if they could talk. Erin is a bit reluctant, but says, "Okay." Mom starts the conversation by apologizing for her reaction earlier. Erin is taken by surprise and gives mom a look as if she was from another planet. Mom continues to explain that the cuts on her arm really scared her earlier and she completely reacted to Erin out of her own fear. When Erin hears the authenticity and love coming from her mom, she starts to cry and apologizes to her mom for what she had done. They are both sitting on Erin's bed, so mom puts her arm around Erin and tells Erin she will not try to stop her anymore. Mom offers to sit with Erin in the future while she cuts so that Erin will not have to be alone anymore. Erin again looks at her mom in complete astonishment. She asks her mom if she is really serious; would she really sit with her and not try to stop her? Mom reassures Erin that she would, told her she would still be scared, and that it would be hard for her, yet she wanted to be with Erin in her pain. Mom explains that that much pain is too much for one person.

Mom and Erin then talk about the cutting and Mom asks Erin to help her understand how it feels when she cuts. Erin explains that even though the cutting hurts, it stops her heart from hurting. Mom holds Erin close and tells her how sorry she is that her heart hurts so badly. Erin opens up and shares that for the past seven years, since she was 7 years old, she has been carrying around the pain surrounding her aunt's death (who was like a mother to Erin). Mom continues to support Erin and love her through her grief and tears.

True story!

(The mother who submitted this story reports that even two years after this connection, her daughter has not self-injured, all as a result of her being able to be there for her daughter instead of being fearful and trying to stop her from cutting.)

Quick Reference
Self-Injury

Remember that self-injury:
- Is an external attempt to soothe an intolerable internal state.
- Is an addictive behavior.
- Is due to a lack of a secure attachment to a parent or caregiver.
- Includes head-banging, carving, scratching, branding, marking, burning, biting, bruising, hitting, picking, and pulling at skin and hair.
- Is an emotionally driven behavior.
- Has a physiological payoff.

When discovering your child has self-injured, recognize she needs you to:
- Check in with yourself to understand the full extent of your reaction.
- Deal with your fears before connecting with her on the issue to be a safe place for her.
- Help interrupt the negative cycle.
- Offer to be in relationship when she has an urge to cut, free of judgment.
- Realize when she comes to you that it has taken a tremendous amount of courage.
- Provide alternatives that are relationally based (doing an activity together to help calm her stress).
- Avoid any type of punishment, consequences, or shame.
- Trust that your calm and loving presence, attention, understanding, and connection is what she needs to shift out of this behavior.

CHAPTER TEN

Defensive Attitudes

■

*"Doesn't the fight for survival also justify
swindle and theft? In self defense, anything goes."*
– Imelda Marcos

In reference to sports, the defense is the part of the team working to prevent the other team from scoring. In military science, defense is the art of protecting and preventing an enemy from attacking. In a court of law, the defense works to prove the truth of the charges against the accused. Hence, defense is a process to protect from harm. For children, this definition to protect from harm holds true, as well.

When children perceive their parents or those in authority to be a threat, either at a conscious or subconscious level, their behaviors take on a stance of protection. They become defensive. The result is a display of defensive behaviors, combined with defensive attitudes.

When Sally's mom gingerly asked her daughter, "Are you sure you're alright, honey...you seem upset." Sally abruptly reacted, "I told you, nothing is wrong! I'm fine! Leave me alone."

Defensive behaviors and attitudes are characterized as being resistant, rude, vindictive, harsh, demeaning, blaming, bossy, arrogant, and abrupt. Interacting with a child who exhibits these types of reactions can, in a very short time, shift the parent out of a place of understanding into a defensive posture of control. After a parent experiences defensive exchanges with a child time and time again, over and over, the parent will eventually get pulled into the vortex of this war zone. These types of constant head banging interactions create a dynamic that leads the parent to become like the child. The parent goes into protection mode and, working from this place of self-preservation, attacks in the same way as the child.

Mom refutes, "Look, Sally! I'm not stupid. I can tell when something is wrong with you!"

Child on the defense, parent on the defense, this relationship is now engaged in a negative feedback loop (see *Beyond Consequences,*

Logic, and Control, Volume 1). Both mom and daughter have the ability to either increase or decrease this negativity. The most important point is that both have the ability to turn this interaction around and create significant positive change at this very moment.

Yet, traditional parenting techniques have focused on keeping the parent in charge to make the child behave differently. These traditional techniques have ignored the emotional charge behind the child's behaviors. When working with defensive attitudes in children, we traditionally have missed asking the two most important questions: **"Why is my child being defensive?"** and **"What is it she is defending?"**

Defensive behaviors and attitudes are learned. Have you ever seen a defensive newborn? Each of us is designed to come into this world complete and able to receive love. We are designed to accept nurturing and connection from our parents. This is our essential condition.

This state of love is not something that is created nor is it something that can be destroyed. It is our life experiences that shift us out of this condition into a place of fear. In this state, our capacity for joy and relationship become constricted and limited because we view the world as dangerous. This perception of danger causes fear, resulting in resistance and defensiveness to whatever or whoever is seen as dangerous. This is especially true when children have life-threatening experiences and, subsequently, view their parents as the source of danger. When you have a child living at this level of resistance, it is about the child living in a place of survival, making it his primary goal to stay alive.

Defensive children have developed this defensiveness as a way to protect themselves from harm and vulnerability. Unfortunately for too many children, they learned at an early age that relationships with adults equate with pain. Whether you as the parent were the unintentional source of that pain or you have taken on the pain of your child's past when he was not with you, as in the case of an adopted or foster child, makes no difference. What you have in front of you is a child who feels the utmost need to keep you at an emotional distance to be safe and prevent history from repeating itself.

If we consider all of this, it becomes quite clear this defensive posture is, in fact, normal human behavior. It is the child's "norm" based on the experiences of his past. It would be your norm if you had experienced the same pain. So the question now becomes, **"How do I help my child regain the lost sense of safety, security, and unconditional love that has been interrupted by fear, pain, and loss in his past?"**

Traditional View

Parenting Techniques - From the lens of the Traditional View, Sally's emotional state (in the example above) would not be a consideration when determining a solution for changing her behaviors. Traditionally, parents have been instructed to implement behavioral strategies, such as removal of privileges, removal of the child's items, and even removal of the parent's connection to get their child to change.

Dr. Michele Borba, parenting author, advises parents, "The best approach to any flippant kid is to refuse to engage. Just simply turn and say, 'When you can talk nice, we can talk.'"[1] Similarly, Dr. Kevin Leman, a bestselling author on parenting and marriage, tells parents to give the request to the child, then turn your back on your child and walk away. He continues to say that you should not tell your child why you are changing your behavior (calling it "your strategy"), and that it is best for your child to figure it out on his own.[2] His belief is that the child will "figure out, sooner or later, that your new, consistent behavior has something to do with the big chip of attitude he's carrying on his shoulder."[3]

The idea with the Traditional View is that the child must not be given anything from the parent until the child turns his attitude around. Dr. Borba advises parents: "Your job is not to turn your behavior around, but his." The approaches are based on the parent staying in control of the interaction with the child.

Therapeutic Interventions – In the literature, traditional therapeutic interventions focus on the function of the therapeutic relationship between the child and the therapist. The majority of therapeutic interventions have the child meet with the therapist one-on-one while the parent waits in the waiting room. Yet, paradoxically, the traditional literature on interventions also emphasizes the importance of the family in the child's life. Emphasis is placed on how family relationships influence the child's identity, perceptions, beliefs, and interactions. Yet, the therapeutic alliance is built between the child and the therapist, not the child and the parent(s).

A New View

The New View recognizes the mask of defensive behaviors and attitudes. If a child (or adult) is acting defensive, there is something much deeper going on below the surface. There is a perceived or anticipated threat driving the child's response against the parent. Working to solely change this behavior and ignoring the issue behind the behavior can have disastrous effects on the parent-child relationship.

Walking away from a child says, *"I have no tolerance for your feelings. Deal with them on your own, then come back when you are happy and regulated."* It is an exceptionally isolating technique that not only hinders the parent-child relationship, but can have life-long damaging effects. When the child is older and needs help from the parent on an issue, the child is less likely to feel emotionally safe to do so.

As children grow up, their issues increase in severity, from not being able to get to the next level in their Gameboy to not knowing whether to do drugs with their friends. Our goal as parents is to create safe, loving, and tolerant relationships with our children in their early years to set the framework for helping them through bigger issues later in life. Leaving our children on their own to "figure out" our strategy is not parenting; it is battling. Walking away from a child does not allow for a connected, trusting, or safe interchange between two human beings.

We need to get back to the basic understanding of defensive attitudes and behaviors. Defensive actions occur when one feels fearful of the other person at any level. Defensive actions are for protecting oneself or avoiding unpleasant ideas, thoughts, or consequences. If we continue to feed more fear into this dynamic by emotionally abandoning our children, giving consequences, or sending our children away to work it out with someone else in therapy, we are only creating more of the same and lose the opportunity to strengthen the parent-child relationship.

> ■
> *Defensive actions occur when one feels fearful of the other person at any level.*
> ■

In such situations, we need to understand the child's fear has him putting all his energy into self-protection instead of self-regulation. **Self-defense has taken the place of self-regulation.** Parenting is about helping and teaching our children how to find balance in their lives, how to regulate their feelings, and how to modulate their internal states, rather than consequencing them for not having the ability to fully master these on their own.

Traditional techniques leave the dysregulated child on his own to find his way back to balance. While some children are able to do this, those with severe behaviors simply cannot; that's the very reason they have severe behaviors. Their internal regulatory systems have been severely compromised; they are unable to regulate overloads of stress and fear. They need the parent to stay in relationship with them to assist them.

What is even more interesting to recognize is that as a child becomes more and more defensive, he becomes less and less able to accurately perceive the motives and feelings of the other person. The motives become exaggerated and more threatening. Clearly, this indicates when a child and parent are in the midst of a heated moment, it is critical the parent be as safe and regulated as possible. Any inclination to the contrary will cause more reaction from the child as the child's defensiveness increases.

The first step is always going to be to diminish the emotional threat that caused the defensive behavior to begin with. Instead of expecting the child to change his behavior in the moment, it is the parent's responsibility to make efforts to change the perception that created the threat. Anything else will only produce more fear and continue to feed the negative neurological feedback loop.

Remember, this defensive behavior is not against you personally. It is an act of self-protection. For some reason, and it will vary for each child, your child is scared of you at that very moment and doesn't feel safe. Do you want to increase this level of fear your child has for you or do you want to become the safe haven he needs to calm his nervous system? Do you want to build your relationship so he does not have to be scared of you in the future? Do you want change or more of the same?

For your child's actual behavior to change, your child must feel safe. The energy and focus your child has on self-protection cannot alter until the level of his emotional safety changes. It is not about changing your child's behavior; it is about changing the way your child perceives you. It takes making yourself different in a way that brings love and acceptance into the interaction with your child. Love, acceptance, and validation create safety.

■

It is not about changing your child's behavior, it is about changing the way your child perceives you.

■

The parent has the power within himself to bring these powerful variables into the "parent + child" equation at any moment of any day. Staying "in charge" or staying "in control" comes not through behavioral techniques as the Traditional View advocates, but from being in a state of love – living from a paradigm of knowing that your loving influence is far more powerful than authoritative control.

Some of this may sound a bit philosophical. Most of us do not have a frame of reference to understand what this looks like "when the rubber hits the road." Most of our parenting programs do not have any perspective of how to do this. Our programs immediately resists and raises the question, *"How does a parent create emotional safety and give her child unconditional love yet at the same time not let the child get away with being ugly and nasty?"*

First it takes shifting your mindset. You have to shift to the understanding that you are not dealing with behaviors; you are dealing with an unexpressed emotional state of fear and overwhelm. It takes trusting that once you reach your child in this emotional state, the behaviors will take care of themselves.

The examples given in this chapter and throughout this book will help you create a new paradigm for parenting. It simply takes opening your mind and heart to trust there is another way. Let us revisit the beginning example with Sally and her mother, but now we will see how mom changes and puts unconditional love into action and creates emotional safety for Sally.

Mom: *"Are you sure you're alright, honey. You seem upset."*

Sally: *"I told you, nothing is wrong! I'm fine! Leave me alone."*

Mom: *"You're right. You did tell me that nothing is wrong. I'm sorry I asked again. I just want you to know that I'm here for you when you're ready."* (Mom validates her daughter, apologizes for coming off as an irritant, and offers unconditional love and to be available to her daughter, under all circumstances, when her daughter is able to connect.)

Sally: *"You always ask me the same stupid questions. I won't tell you because you don't really care anyway."*

Mom: *"Wow. That must feel really bad not to have a mom who really cares about you."* (Mom is validating Sally's perception because that is Sally's reality. Mom does care but she does not need to jump into the ring of fire to defend that she cares more than Sally will ever understand.)

Sally: *"You don't know what it feels like and don't try this psychobabble stuff on me!"*

Mom: *"No, I don't know what it feels like and I'm not going to try to pretend to know what it feels like. But I want to be able to understand you and to be here for you."*

Sally: *"You'll never understand me!"*

Mom: (Mom simply stays present with her daughter, not saying a word but sits down in a chair near her daughter. Mom is placing herself in a more physically safe posture, instead of standing over Sally. Mom stays conscious of her body position and facial expressions, working to be an inviting and safe place for Sally.)

Sally: *"No one understands me! You, dad, my teachers! No one! Everybody just gets mad at me and expects me to do things their way."*

Mom: *"You're right. We haven't taken the time to really listen to you and understand you better. It must be awfully lonely."*

Sally: *"I hate you. I hate dad. I hate everybody. I'm better off being alone!"*

Mom: (Mom reflects that Sally has been using this defensive attitude to do exactly that, to be alone, and worse, it has been working.) *"It probably feels safer to be alone."*

Sally: *"It is better than talking to you guys and only getting shit from you."*

Mom: (Mom realizes this is the longest conversation they have had in months, so she refrains from correcting Sally's profanity at this moment.) *"Well, that does make sense."*

Mom and Sally are finally communicating. This is the first step in the process. While Sally's attitude is not ideal at this point, we have to see this relationship did not get strained overnight so neither will it be fixed in one flash. Mom was able to simply stop and allow Sally to express herself...a monumental step for the two of them.

If you are struggling with the fact that Sally was nasty to her mother, used profanity, and told her mother she hated her, you are focused on the outcome, not the process. This can be a difficult shift to make. The goal in the beginning is to create connection and safety, knowing the behavior is only a byproduct of the relationship. Connection and safety was accomplished in this exchange. That is to be celebrated because these two elements must be in place before a child will have the capacity to even consider a parent's request to make behavioral changes.

Here's the next step. An hour later or perhaps later that evening, Mom can sit with Sally and tell her how glad she was to have had this conversation earlier in the day. Mom can express how grateful she is to finally understand her daughter and how much she appreciates Sally's willingness to communicate this information with her. Additionally, Mom can simply request, in a loving way, that she and Sally work in the future to use appropriate language (because I'm certain that Mom in the past has let out a few words of profanity of her own in moments of complete frustration). Mom can express how sad it is when Sally uses mean words against her. Mom can take ownership of the fact that, in the past, she was not listening to Sally and the only way Sally knew to get her mom's attention was to communicate with this negative tone and profanity. They both can make the commitment to listen to each other with openness and work to communicate their needs in appropriate ways.

This is the true definition of discipline – to teach. As stated earlier, defensive attitudes and behaviors for traumatized children are learned from the child's life experiences of adults being irresponsible, whether intentionally or unintentionally. It therefore correlates that it is the responsibility of the adults in the child's life to teach new behaviors and attitudes that will equip the child for success. It would be yet another act of irresponsibility on the parent's part to force the child into figuring out how to change on his own, as advised by the Traditional View.

Defensive attitudes are the only way many children know to create a wall of safety around them, protecting themselves from the injustices of being vulnerable, helpless, powerless, scared, and misunderstood. Children will only change their behaviors when they feel safe and capable of managing the world around them without this behavior. This is the power of putting love (through patience, listening, understanding, tolerance, and acceptance) back into the child's world. It provides safety and allows children to return back to their original essential condition. **Love is the only communication with another that consistently works all the time.**

■

Children will only change their behaviors when they feel safe and capable of managing the world around them without this behavior.

■

Parenting Example: Defensive Attitude

Scenario:

Alison, 16 years old, blames everything on someone or something else. It is never her fault or her responsibility. Tonight, Alison's mom needed her to help out by setting the table. Her mom asked Alison about 15 minutes ago to come and help but there was no sign of Alison. As mom was busy finishing dinner, Alison's brother, Jimmy, walked into the kitchen so mom asked him to set the table instead. When the family was ready to sit down for dinner, mom finally just called across the house for Alison. She still did not respond so mom stopped everything and went to summon Alison.

Traditional View

Mom: Mom opens Alison's door and says *"Alison, what are you doing? Dinner is ready and I asked you 15 minutes ago to help out and set the table."*

Alison: *"I couldn't come help you. My teacher didn't give me enough time on this project so now I'm crammed to get it finished!"*

Mom: *"Well, it's dinner time and everybody is waiting for you."*

Alison: *"I have to get this done for tomorrow. What, do you want me to fail?"*

Mom: *"Don't turn this around and blame me. I needed you to come help me. I've been cooking dinner and the least you could do is have the courtesy to set the table. Besides, you've had weeks to work on this project."*

Alison: *"Well, you didn't say exactly when you needed me to set the table. I was going to do it. Geez!"*

Mom: *"Alison, you're being very rude and inconsiderate. When you can talk to me in a nice tone, then we'll have something to discuss. Dinner is ready and your father and brother are sitting and waiting for you. You need to go sit down at the table now."*

Alison: *"Jimmy could have a least told me dinner was ready. I bet he even played 'good boy' and set the table for you!"*

Mom: *"Yes, he filled in for you so I fully expect you to thank him when you sit down at the table."*

Alison: *"He does stuff like this all the time, just to make me look bad!"*

Mom: *"Alison, you created this. You need to take responsibility and stop blaming everyone, especially Jimmy, for your shortcomings."*

Alison: *"Oh, so I'm just one big fat shortcoming, now! If that's what you think of me, then I'm not coming to dinner!"*

Mom: *"Are you done being defensive, yet? Because I'm not going to allow you to disrespect me and manipulate my words like this anymore."* (Mom turns to leave.)

Alison: *"Fine! Leave so I can get some peace and quiet. And by the way, when did you go to 'Meanest Mom on Earth' school, anyway?"*

Mom: Rolling her eyes, mom leaves to go eat dinner. She is irritated and feeling defeated and helpless. Anything she says to her daughter gets twisted and turned back onto her as if it is all her fault. Yet, she knows that Alison will learn a good lesson when she does not finish her project and receives a low grade. Mom rejoices, *"let the consequences fall as they may."*

A New View

Mom: Mom begins reflecting about how she is feeling unappreciated, disrespected, and simply worn out, hungry, and tired. Mom works to shift herself into a loving state to connect with Alison. Mom knocks on Alison's door.

Alison: *"What!!! I'm busy working on my project!!!"*

Mom: *"Are you okay, honey? I thought you were going to come help me so we could get dinner on the table."* Mom begins to open the door, peeking in to see Alison, yet mom is careful to respect her daughter's privacy.

Alison: *"I can't come help you. My teacher didn't give me enough time on this project so now I'm crammed to get it finished!"*

Mom: *"You sound really stressed out right now, sweetheart."*

Alison: *"Of course I'm stressed out. You'd be stressed out too if you had this lousy teacher!"*

Mom: Mom knows Alison was given enough time for this project but she procrastinated until the last minute because she got overwhelmed and tried to ignore it as a way to deal with it. Yet, she knows pointing out she had adequate time would only feed this negative communication. Instead, mom says, *"I had no idea you were under such a deadline."*

Alison: *"I told you earlier I had this due. You never listen to me!"*

Mom: *"I'm sorry, honey, it just didn't register with me how much work you had to do tonight."*

Alison: Alison feels her mother's connection and authenticity. She begins to lift the defensive wall, *"I just don't know how I'm going to get this all done, mom!"*

Mom: Mom moves in closer and sits down next to her daughter. *"How about you take a quick break to eat dinner and I'll come back with you to see how we can tackle this together tonight?"*

Alison: *"I'm so scared I'm going to fail and you and dad will be so disappointed in me!*

Mom: *"I'm so sorry you didn't feel like you could come tell me before now how this was stressing you out."* Mom pauses and just holds Alison in her arms. *"Honey, we love you and your grades don't determine how much we love or don't love you. All we ever ask is that you do your best . . . (pause).......Take a break with me and we'll get this done afterwards. There is always a way."*

Alison sits down to dinner with her family and reconnects after a stressful day. She and mom stay up well past midnight to complete the project. Mom recognizes that Alison simply got overwhelmed by this project and was unable to schedule her time effectively. Mom helped her out this time because she realized Alison needed more coaching on how to manage her time and work through her fears of not being good enough. The next day, they sat down together and talked about how it could be done differently next time. They worked out a new system to follow for all projects in the future. For each project Alison had from that moment forward, she needed less and less of mom's help until eventually, Alison learned how to handle the completion of projects solely on her own. Additionally, the more Alison was met with understanding, patience, and tolerance from her parents, the more her defensive attitude in all interactions dissipated.

True story!

Quick Reference
Defensive Attitude

Remember that a defensive child is:
- Perceiving those in authority to be a threat.
- A child working to protect himself.
- Being stirred up by something much deeper that needs to be addressed.
- Working to avoid unpleasant thoughts or feelings.
- Unable to regulate an overload of stress and fear.
- Distorted in his ability to perceive you as safe.

When communicating with a defensive child, recognize he needs you to:
- Stop taking his defensive behavior personally.
- Understand he will only change his behavior when he feels emotionally safe and understood.
- Diminish the emotional or physical threat within yourself.
- Help him reach the fear and overwhelm driving the defensive behavior.
- Give him emotional space to express himself, no matter how this communication comes out in the beginning.
- Let him have a voice while you ignore the accusations he makes against you, refrain from correcting, and simply stay present and listen to the level of pain underneath all the above.
- Teach him how to communicate and how to interact with you in a more positive way, only after he is calm and regulated.

CHAPTER ELEVEN

No Conscience

■

*"Your conscience is the measure of the honesty
of your selfishness. Listen to it carefully."*
– Richard Bach

The "official conscience" of Pinnochio, Jiminy Cricket, is famous for saying, "Let your conscience be your guide." Our conscience is the inner voice that senses what is right or wrong in our behavior or motives. It is the part of us that compels us toward right action. Conscience is developed through the context of relationships.

Children perceived to have no conscience are often described as feeling no empathy for others and being involved in persistent and serious patterns of breaking rules and harming others. Practitioners' clinical notes often state, "Client lacks a conscience and a real capacity for relationships."

Parents are often told by professionals: "Your child does not have a conscience" and the professional hands the parent an official diagnosis of conduct disorder (CD) or reactive attachment disorder (RAD), or both. Additionally, well-meaning professionals, unaware of their own fear of the child, often point out the grim outcome if the child does not develop his conscience. Reminders of adults such as Ted Bundy, Jeffrey Dahmer, Myra Hindley, Jack the Ripper, and other infamous cold-blooded, conscienceless killers all too often find their way into articles, books, and Internet websites regarding children perceived to lack a conscience.

A grandmother once called me in tears, seeking help for her 7-year-old granddaughter she was raising. She had been working regularly with a therapist for over a year. After a series of incidents by the child, the therapist decided these were indicative of this child not having a conscience. Engulfed in fear and terror, the grandmother sobbed on the phone:

"Peggy (the therapist) said my granddaughter, Julia, doesn't have a conscience. She's going to grow up hurting people. I don't know what to do. I can't give her back...I'm the only stability she has in her life. But, I can't stay committed to raising a serial killer."

Several months earlier, I had spoken with this grandmother – she had attended one of my local parenting courses. At the time of this earlier interaction, I had sensed the "attachment" therapy she was receiving was fear-based and adding to the stress in the home instead of strengthening her relationship with her granddaughter. I had to work to regulate myself as the anger began to erupt inside of me, knowing all of this could have been prevented and that much of it was the therapist's own fear that had been the catalyst for this conclusion of no conscience. This therapist had been working with this family for a length of time and she was realizing that no progress was being made. Instead of looking at the model of treatment as the culprit, she automatically turned it onto the child. The shift from working to help this child to blaming this child was challenging my own nervous system. So, I sat there, breathing deeply as I felt the pain and fear of the grandmother cascading through the phone line.

Traditional View

Professionals working with children with severe behaviors have deemed it appropriate to correlate characteristics of children with "no conscience" to the characteristics of psychopaths.[1] Books designed to be resources for parents have lists of infamous people who have committed atrocities[2], even listing statistics such as "in New York alone, since 1986, there have been at least seven occurrences of adoptees murdering their adoptive parents."[3]

These children have been described as having no conscience, a defective conscience[4], or a lack of conscience[5]. Other descriptors are often noted as "lack of empathy for others,"[6] "has no inner voice to do the right thing and stay on the moral path,"[7] and "their conscience is entirely absent."[8]

Stories included in books describe children with trauma histories as having a sense of delight when seeing others get hurt or when causing pain.[9] They state remorse only comes when the child is caught and exposed. Children are seen to be cold and never genuinely sorry. The traditional belief is these children do not even care when they hurt their siblings and the child "truly does not care about right or wrong."[10] Parents find themselves reading descriptions in books describing their child as "a self-centered, callous, and remorseless person profoundly lacking in empathy and the ability to form warm emotional relationships with others, a person who functions without restraints of conscience."[11]

Other books examining the behaviors of psychopaths explain their lack of remorse or guilt is associated with an uncanny ability to rationalize and justify their behavior. They describe them as refusing to take personal responsibility for their behaviors, no matter how shocking and hurtful they have been to family and friends. They simply are not able to "walk in the shoes" of others. Even beyond this, it is explained they often twist the situation around and portray themselves as the victim, describing how badly *they* were hurt.[12]

Traditional literature delivers a pessimistic, disheartening message that treatment for these individuals is ineffective and falls short of dealing with these children.[13] Little hope is offered; only fear is given. After describing all the pitfalls of traditional therapies in his book, "High Risk Children Without a Conscience," Dr. Ken Magid concludes, *"the parent with an unattached child faces a mighty challenge. Unfortunately the therapist who sees the APD (antisocial personality disorder) patient is in the same boat."*[14] Others warn that children with the childhood mental health diagnosis of oppositional defiant disorder, conduct disorder, and/or reactive attachment disorder is a compelling concern for severe aggression and criminal behavior in adulthood.[15]

A New View

These descriptions presented in the Traditional View leave parents overwhelmed and fearful of the future, not only for their child, but also for the safety of themselves and their entire family. This information has the power to triangulate and distance parents from their children – children who are acting this way because of the separation they are experiencing to begin with. Only more of the same is created.

We must ask the right questions: What is driving this behavior? What is preventing a child from behaving from a conscious, rational place?

Following the principles of the *Beyond Consequences* model, we must go back to looking beyond the behavior. We must ask the right questions: What is driving this behavior? What is preventing a child from behaving from a conscious, rational place?

When we are in a place of survival, it is that we can't have a conscience, not that we don't have a conscience. We are in a place of survival...the only person we have concern for is ourself. At that point, everybody is a threat to our existence. Nobody matters except us to prevent being hurt, injured, or even killed.

> *On May 30, 1999, in Minsk, Belarus, 2,500 fans gathered to see Russian band Mango Mango at an outdoor festival. As rain and hail began to fall, people rushed for the shelter of a subway station, trampling 53 people. This was the largest disaster ever at a music festival.*

This disaster in Belarus is a excellent example of what happens to our conscience when we become overwhelmed and frightened. Did these thousands of concertgoers who ran for cover lack a conscience? Was it just a coincidence that all 2,500 people gathering together had no conscience or no inner voice directing their moral behavior? No. Of course they had a conscience. Yet, they could only access their conscience when they felt safe and calm and in an internal space of happiness and joy. It was when the rain and hail came pouring down that they shifted into a place of fear. The threat of being injured triggered their primal survival reaction and the only concern was for themselves, no one else.

In such events, the reptilian and limbic brains become activated (as discussed in Chapter 2). The brain stem, located in the reptilian region, mediates our core regulatory functions such as body temperature, heart rate, respiration, and blood pressure. The limbic area handles emotional responses that guide our behavior. The top part of the brain, the neocortex, where complex and rational thinking, planning skills, and deliberate decision making occurs, is literally shut off during times of extreme heightened arousal.[16] In cases such as this concert tragedy, those caught in terror were acting according to their emotional responses from the lower areas, the more primal areas, of their brains. Their higher-level thinking was inaccessible. At that moment, it became about them with the focus on getting to a place of safety, no matter the cost.

In his book, *The Biology of Belief,* Dr. Bruce Lipton states *"when it comes to sheer neurological processing abilities, the subconscious mind is millions of times more powerful than the conscious mind"* and *"the actions of the subconscious mind are reflexive in nature and are not governed by reason or thinking."* [17] In times of heightened stress, our actions are automatic neurological responses. It is actually perfectly normal to act this way! What a relief. Your child is not doing anything outside his biological programming.

A child who appears to lack a conscience is a child who is in a pervasive state of trying to survive at a life-or-death level. This is a child at his most raw and core place of survival, unable to express empathy or concern for others' wellbeing. When you are dealing with children with traumatic histories, children who have been labeled as not having a conscience, you are working with children operating mainly out of their reptilian brains.

Unfortunately, however, professionals have labeled these children as having a "defective conscience" or as a child who "lacks empathy." This has been utterly misleading and stems from a grave misunderstanding of human behavior along with a total dismissal of neuroscience. This type of information is incredibly damaging to parents and, ultimately, to children. Parents seek help from professionals, feeling helpless and hopeless, only to be given information projecting disastrous outcomes. Having no other place to turn, parents begin to believe this information. When we consider the power of the mind, we now know your belief becomes your reality. "Your beliefs are like filters on a camera, changing how you see the world."[18] Here's a story about the power of beliefs:

Many years ago, a man was traveling across the country by sneaking from one freight train to the next. One night he climbed into what he thought was a boxcar. He closed the door, which automatically locked shut and trapped him inside. When his eyes adjusted to the light, he realized he was inside a refrigerated box-car, and he became aware of the intense, freezing cold. He called for help and pounded on the door, but all the noise he made from inside the car failed to attract anyone's attention. After many hours of struggle, he lay down on the floor of the railroad car.

As he tried to fight the freezing cold, he scratched a message on the floor explaining his unfortunate, imminent death. Late the next day, repairmen from the railroad opened the door and found the dead man inside. Though the man had all the appearances of having frozen to death, the truth was the repairmen had come to fix the broken refrigerator unit in that car. Most likely the temperature of the railroad car had never fallen below 50 degrees during the night. The man had died because he thought he was freezing to death.[19]

If you have a child who appears to have no conscience, expand your brain, your heart, and your soul at this very moment. Take some deep breaths. The only way to shift your paradigm after someone has told you your child does not have a conscience is to open the space within you to hear something different. It is terrible to have any child be given this label. When a parent is told his child does not have a conscience, an automatic deep state of fear emerges because attached to this statement are negative thoughts of the future (e.g., *"Your child is going to become a serial killer, a thief – a criminal!"*).

Embrace the fear and realize children who are labeled as having no conscience are children in a pervasive state of terror. What this means is that your child is saying:

"I am terrified and I have to protect myself every moment of the day; everything in my life is a threat to me. When you come towards me, I have to attack you because I believe you are going to hurt me."

But you are thinking, *"I'm not trying to kill my child. I'm as calm and safe as I can be. Certainly my child knows I'm the parent. How can he be in survival?"* It takes looking beyond your own perception. Due to early experiences, your child perceives you as a threat. This perception is based from his blueprints of the past – based from what he has learned from interactions with others. "Our responses to environmental stimuli are indeed controlled by perceptions, but not all of our learned perceptions are accurate. Not all snakes are dangerous!" [20]

So to punish a child for his dysregulation and his "no conscience" driven behavior, we do nothing for the child's long-term healing. Parents need to create emotional space and safety by avoiding fear-based parenting to help settle his nervous system and change his perception. Parents must become more aware and conscious of how easily the child becomes threatened. More importantly, it is beneficial for parents to move out of the black-and-white interpretation that their child is "always" without empathy or "never" has a conscience. It is our fear preventing us from realizing our children do have moments when they are regulated and able to access their conscience. It is our fear distorting our interpretation when children are being kind and empathetic.

Continuing from the earlier story of the grandmother whose therapist described her granddaughter as having no conscience:

"But how can this be? I'm terrified of what my therapist said and I am so confused. Just last week, I was sick and Julia was so tender and sweet – at least I thought she was. Julia brought me a glass of orange juice and whispered a sweet get well wish. I thought she was finally developing empathy but if she doesn't have a conscience, that means it was all fake. She was simply manipulating me and being nice on her own terms!"

When parents and caregivers believe their children have no conscience, that becomes the framework from which they interpret their child's actions. In the case with this grandmother, the fear of her granddaughter growing up to be a criminal without a conscience shifted her perspective. The reality is that Julia was able to be kind and thoughtful at that moment. Her physiological system was calm and her amygdala was not pumping out neurotransmitters putting her into a hyper-aroused, fearful state. Julia had the capacity to think clearly enough to select orange juice, which has Vitamin C. She didn't grab tea or lemonade, but made a deliberate choice to bring what her grandmother needed. This is far from manipulative and shows a child who was making a conscious choice to be helpful and kind.

Siblings. The issue of "no conscience" often arises in sibling issues. Many children feel so threatened by their siblings that they lash out at them, sometimes brutally. Shifting the perspective to see the child is reacting from fear instead of maliciously premeditating the act (yes, it can look that way!), the parent's response can then work to calm and secure the child. The behavior is stemming from not feeling secure in the family system, so the parental response needs to be in alignment with this.

When Bobby comes to sit down at the dinner table and spouts off mean innuendos towards his sister, the parent needs to realize that due to negative repetitious conditioning and past experiences, Bobby goes into a heightened state when he gathers with his family. As the parent stays mindful of Bobby's insecurities (thus degrading his sister to heighten his importance and to attempt to secure his foundation in the family), the parent can respond differently this time. Instead of saying, *"Don't say those things to your sister, Bobby!"* this time the parent can simply pull her chair closer to her child, gently put her arm around him, and say, *"I'm so glad you're here with us."*

To do this through the lens of love, it takes the parent embracing her fear, moving through her need to control the situation, shifting outside of her need to make everything perfect at dinner time, and seeing this child differently. It takes seeing far beyond what mental health professionals have told the parent about the child having no conscience. The child is reacting from a place of fear rather than a place of mal intent.

Teaching the Life Lesson After the Event. When a child feels threatened, his behavior will be reactive in nature. It is important for parents not to approach their child about the negative event in the moment. Jody, a 14-year-old foster child hits her younger sister, then fervently says, *"I don't care. I'll hit whoever I want to hit and I'll hit them whenever I want to hit them."* At the behavioral level, she is demonstrating a lack of concern for others, a lack of remorse, a lack of empathy – a lack of conscience. We must realize that confronting her in the heat of the moment and then telling her, *"That is horrible. You don't have a conscience, I can't believe you. You're going to kill somebody someday."* is only increasing the threat.

To help calm her amygdala and help her to shift into a place of loving regulation, ignore her behavior, but don't ignore her. In this example with Jody, the foster parent should first attend to the hurt child to help her calm down, saying, *"I'm sorry I didn't make it safe for you, sweetheart. Jody is really scared right now and I'm going to go help her so that everyone is okay."* Then, the foster parent should immediately go to Jody and say in a loving tone, *"Come over with me, honey. Sit down, you must be feeling really stressed. You actually look really angry and when you're angry I know you don't feel safe. Sit with me for a few minutes. You're not in trouble."*

Negative Thinking Creates Negative Outcomes. When parents operate from the perspective their child has no conscience, they often assume the child took pleasure in the negative event. When such negative events fall outside the parents' perceptual understanding or are clouded by negative predictions, like the child becoming a serial killer, parents automatically determine these events to be indicators of the worst possible outcomes. Parents see their child as a threat, which only perpetuates the fear and insecurity driving this behavior from

■

Who would want to snuggle up at night with a potential serial killer?

■

the start. Additionally, it keeps parents distanced from their child and constricted in their ability to bond with the child. Who would want to snuggle up at night with a potential serial killer?

The *Beyond Consequences* New View offers parents the truth: *"This child did this because he was scared. He is absolutely terrified and doesn't know he is going to be okay."* The child needs the parent to bring him in close, free of judgment, free of shame and with total acceptance and understanding. The moment of the incident is the prime moment to create connection...it is the moment of healing. It is a moment of teaching for the child to experience that she is safe, secure, and loved unconditionally.

Later that day or evening, the moral lesson of not hurting others and the household boundaries can be set. Learning can only happen when the body system is calm and regulated. The parent then has the opportunity to discuss the event: *"Honey, when you hit your sissy, it makes me sad. It tells me you're scared and that you think I love her more. I need you to know you do not have to injure your sister to have my love. I love you and I will never stop loving you. Your sister cannot change my love for you, ever."* The parent can then invite the child to come and get her the next time the child feels threatened by the sibling. *"The next time you feel like you have to hurt your sister, I need you to come get me so I can help you feel better."*

Selfishness is defined "as the act of placing one's own needs or desires above the needs or desires of others." [20] The more selfish state you are in, the less conscience you have available, just as the beginning quote of this chapter stated ("...your conscience is the measure of your selfishness"). It simply comes down to how safe, secure, and loved you are feeling.

This is indeed a gauge for parents to understand their children. If a child is placing his needs above the needs or desires of another person, the gauge is reading "survival." The higher functioning levels of the brain that allow a child to "have a conscience" are still present; they simply aren't accessible at that moment. Parenting your child to secure your relationship with him, going beyond the behaviors by providing safety and security, will allow your child the healing experiences he needs to develop empathy and shift out of feeling like he needs to fight for his life. In fact, once children are given this type of environment to heal, many actually develop more empathy than their peers because they have been down to the depths of their souls. They know what it feels like to hurt and they know the pain of helplessness. They are able to tap into their intuition and develop an amazing ability to relate to and understand people.

Parenting Example: No Conscience

Scenario: Sasha was adopted from the Ukraine at the age of 8 and is now 13 years old. On Mother's Day, his parents discovered he had cornered his brother, also 13 years old, and pounded him with rocks in the woods behind their house. In the past, when confronted with such behavioral acts, Sasha initially showed no remorse or empathy. Yet, upon being caught and knowing he cannot convince his parents otherwise, he becomes exceptionally remorseful. This pattern has repeated itself within this family for the past five years.

Traditional View

Sasha is now 13 years old and this family is running out of time to change this child. The parents MUST BE IN CONTROL and take immediate action. Sasha has violated the values and rules of this household, so he needs a consequence to learn how his actions affect others. Sasha will be assigned numerous chores to earn his way back into the family and to feel the same pain he inflicted on his brother.

Sasha's parents know in their hearts that Sasha's current behavior and lack of remorse will lead to serious adult issues, so they sought the help of a trusted professional. After evaluating Sasha, the professional explained to the parents the definition of "sociopath." The professional explained that Sasha fits this definition to a "T." After three months of treatment, the parents were told by this professional, "Psychotherapy can do wonders with mental health disorders but can do nothing for character disorders. Psychotherapy also requires that the client wants to change and that the client recognizes there is a problem. Sasha doesn't show any sign of recognizing a need to change or that there is a problem. Therapy is only becoming a place for him to hone his manipulation skills. At this point, there is nothing more I can do to try to help Sasha."

His parents begin researching for ways to fix Sasha. The resources they find conclude that "attempts to deflect the person from his or her psychopathic pattern early in life generally have not been successful." [22] His parents decide he is unsafe in the home and the other children are in danger of being hurt. Sasha will be sent to a residential treatment center so the rest of the family can get back to a place of peace and safety.

A New View

The parents first realize this is a difficult day for Sasha. It is Mother's Day. Mother's Day for adopted children is a reminder of the most profound loss they will ever experience – the loss of their birthmother. Even though it is a day to be focused on Sasha's mom, she realizes this day is difficult for her son and he needs his parents to understand his internal turmoil.

His parents realize if he is beating up his brother and showing no remorse, even after five years of being in their home, their son continues to live in a state of survival. He is feeling threatened by his brother, especially because they are the same age. He feels he has to protect himself and fight to stay alive in this family. The parents realize they all have been engaged in a negative feedback loop of fear for far too long. To interrupt this cycling, Sasha needs to feel safe, protected, and understood. The only way for him to learn empathy and develop his conscience is for his parents to model it for him.

Sasha's parents begin the process of building a stronger, more loving, safer relationship with their son. They refrain from lectures of shame filled with anger and disapproval. Sasha's parents go to him and begin to take responsibility: *"Sasha, it looks like you were feeling really unsafe with your brother. We never realized how scared you've been in this family and how you've felt like an outcast from your siblings. We're here to keep you safe, son, and we're going to start doing things differently from this point forward."*

After three months of parenting in the *Beyond Consequences* model and modeling empathy, understanding, tolerance, and patience with Sasha, his parents write, *"When we were heavy into using consequences, Sasha just learned how to get better about not being caught! Not a lot of conscience building was happening, or not the type we had hoped for. We've gone so much further in building empathy, remorse, etc., when we simply work on our relationship with him. It has taken becoming a safe place for him and being able to talk openly with him. He has been more trusting and receptive to what we've talked about and we have modeled our behaviors to where we have seen his conscience grow. We know on the inside he isn't dead – he is a beautiful blossoming young man. We have our moments when he gets scared and stressed, but we have seen first-hand that conscience building comes naturally when focusing on building the relationship. Approval and love go 100 times farther in building his conscience than anything else."*

True story!

Quick Reference
No Conscience

Remember that a child showing no signs of a conscience:
- Is in a state of survival.
- Has his reptilian and limbic brains activated, leaving his rational brain (the neocortex) inaccessible.
- Is unable to express empathy because he is fighting for his life.
- Perceives everyone, especially his parents and siblings, as a threat.
- May act as if he has to injure his sibling to be alright in the family system.
- Does not inherently know he is safe and going to be okay.

When discovering your child is showing signs of no conscience, recognize he needs you to:
- Stop fearing he is going to grow up to be a psychopath or criminal.
- Shift out of the fear of the future to be connected with him in the present.
- Help create a safe environment for him.
- Stop adding more fear into him through consequences and punishment.
- Understand his level of survival and feelings of terror – sheer terror.
- Model empathy for him.
- "Get into his shoes" so he can learn how to "get into the shoes" of others.
- Trust that conscience building comes naturally when focused on building your relationship with him.

CHAPTER TWELVE

Homework Battles

■

*"I like a teacher who gives you something to
take home to think about besides homework."*
– Lily Tomlin

*"If they don't learn to do their homework now, they'll never
make it in college."* These were the exact words of a teacher when
speaking to a parent about the necessity of homework. She was ada-
mant the children in her classroom learn to be responsible and self-
disciplined. While it might be possible to fathom this statement coming from a high school teacher or perhaps a middle school teacher, it
is hard to believe these were the words of a kindergarten teacher. That
would equate to the absolute need for a 5-year-old to go home after a
full six hours of school and do more work.

Homework has become the norm for children attending school
from kindergarten through high school. Homework is viewed as an
intellectual discipline to establish good study habits and develop good
character. Teachers use it to ease time constraints on the amount of
material that can be covered in class and to supplement and reinforce
the lessons covered in school. Homework is
intended to foster student initiative, independence, and responsibility.

While the thoughts and ideas behind
homework are all well intended and sound
logical and reasonable, do they actually play
out in the reality of most school-age children?
If you took a video camera into 100,000 homes
after school and filmed what was happening
in these homes during homework time, what
would you see: intellectual discipline or rebellious chaos?

As many parents would testify, you
would see the latter – rebellious chaos. In fact,
you would see rebellious chaos unmatched
by any other activity children are asked to
perform. You would see children yelling and

■

*If you took a video
camera into 100,000
homes after school
and filmed what was
happening in these
homes during
homework time,
what would you see:
intellectual
discipline or
rebellious chaos?*

■

tearing up their homework. You would see pencils flying, books being slammed, and tearful cries and threats of: *"I hate you. I'm not doing this homework and you can't make me."* Most children would rather go to the dentist than do their homework! In addition to seeing children exhibiting negative behaviors, you would also see parents hitting their window of stress tolerance. You would see parents reverting to being 2-year-olds as they reach new levels of exasperation. And all of this would be in the name of "learning."

Articles and books with new coined phrases such as "homework stress" and "homework wars" are available for parents seeking answers to this dilemma. Most expert advice centers on how to get children to do their work, and they are focused on the outcome of children walking into class with their homework in hand to turn in to their teacher.

These coined phrases, *homework stress* and *homework wars*, warrant a moment to consider and explore. They are an interesting combination of words: homework/stress and homework/war. The juxtaposition of these two words can in no way foster our children's love for learning. First, we know from scientific research that stress causes short-term memory loss. An over-secretion of stress hormones adversely affects the brain and can prevent the brain from laying down a new memory or accessing already existing memories.[1] No one can learn when he is stressed out. Second, war is about winning, which implies someone will lose. When homework becomes a battle, everybody loses; there are no winners. Learning is supposed to be fun, not a conflict or fight for survival.

Traditional View

> *"At ABC School, homework is assigned every evening in every subject. This includes weekends, holidays, and vacation days. If a parent is told or believes that their son or daughter does not have nightly homework, instead of accepting an explanation from the student, please call the school immediately! The preparation of homework is a shared responsibility – the student-parent-teacher. Please call the principal as soon as possible if you sense any kind of problem concerning the homework. Also, where homework is not completed or is inadequately prepared, parents will be called by the teacher. Continued failure to prepare and turn in homework will be considered a deficiency that will affect the student's final grade."*

These are the words taken directly from a homework policy of a school in the state of New York. This view of homework reflects many schools throughout the United States, both public and private. In the Traditional View, schools typically use strict policies and procedures to ensure the completion of out-of-school assignments. In this example, a sense of urgency to call the principal (the person with the highest degree of control) is given to the parents to correct a child not adhering to the policy.

Parental guidelines for helping children with homework in the Traditional View focus on many logistical procedures to follow at home. Recommendations include monitoring television viewing, establishing a specific homework time, planning a homework schedule with the child, and allowing free time only when assignments are completed.

Educators place a tremendous amount of emphasis around the lesson of responsibility and homework. The two are tied closely together, as if the two are one and the same. *"Children need to know early on that homework is a responsibility; everything else is a privilege."* Homework in this traditional perspective is seen to take precedence over extracurricular activities such as violin or piano lessons, karate, or other social activities. One educator from Brown University, who represents the mindset of so many of our children's educators, says that getting homework done is the single most important job a child has. She states, *"Parents who put extracurricular activities ahead of it [homework] have it backwards."*[2]

Parenting experts, especially those specializing in working with oppositional children and children diagnosed with RAD, stress the importance of making certain that homework must be 100 percent of the child's responsibility beginning as early as the first grade. It is thought that children diagnosed with reactive attachment disorder (RAD) or oppositional defiant disorder (ODD) seek battles. Thus, when the parent engages in a battle over homework, the child will automatically fight it and nothing will be accomplished. Instead, the Traditional View recommends the parent not interact in the homework process and as the child learns the natural consequences of not doing homework is an automatic zero or F, the child will move toward the improvement by putting out effort. This process of putting out effort for himself is seen as a way to build a child's self-esteem. Additionally, *"they must believe the truth, that an education is vital to their success in their adult life, and that their brain must have exercise to develop properly."*[3]

Professionals helping families struggling through homework

issues traditionally suggest writing a contract between the parent and the child. The contract includes both the parent's and the child's participation and approval. A copy is then kept in the child's file at school and a copy is given to the family to post at home.[4]

Books written on helping children with their homework suggest the parent help only when there is an absence of anger or frustration. Dr. Charles Fay suggests the parent help only when the child can describe what the teacher said. This response from the parent is to ensure the child understands it is important to pay attention to teachers. Other books instruct parents to hold rigid boundaries of "work before play," with no exceptions. Parents are to enforce these rules "matter of factly."[5]

Some experts working from the traditional perspective recommend that to prevent dependency, avoid falling into the habit of sitting at the table as your child does his homework. *"If your child needs you to sit with him, something is wrong."*[6] This view also stresses the parent should not do the homework for their children, saying that when this happens, they miss the point. *"Homework is meant to be practice. That means you are allowed to make mistakes."*[7]

A New View

The Brain. As previously discussed, the prefrontal cortex (located in the neocortex) gives us higher cognitive abilities such as alertness, attention, planning, memory, and the ability to regulate appropriate social behavior (i.e., emotional and impulse control). In children, this part of the brain is still developing and will not finish developing until they are at least 25 years old. Research over the last 10 years clearly shows stress impairs this part of the brain in adults and children. [8] Plainly stated, this means when children become stressed out, they cannot think clearly. Their prefrontal cortex, the thinking brain, is inaccessible. Asking children to do homework during this time is a set-up for failure and frustration.

The suggestions listed in the Traditional View do not account for this finding. The solutions given are cognitively based. They assume the child is in a position to think clearly through his choices. Yet in many cases, nothing could be further from the truth. If a child cannot think clearly, policies and procedures will make no sense and certainly have no impact on motivating a child. In fact, policies and procedures typically create more stress and negatively impact a child's sense of motivation.

Cause and effect thinking requires upper-level brain capacity. The Traditional View assumes a child who fails because he has not done his homework will be able to correlate the two together and come to a logical conclusion. It assumes a child will understand that to pass, he must study and do homework, and motivation will be established.

Unfortunately, for children who are already stressed out, failing only breeds more stress and more overwhelm. Failure will not motivate such a child to take action. It will only widen and deepen his internal pit of overwhelm, keeping him trapped and feeling more worthless.

The Traditional View also fails to consider a child's emotional state. It views children as logical machines or computers and suggests parents respond in this mechanical way, as well. Children do not operate by "if-then statements." An if-then statement is just what the name implies. It is a statement that proves if something happens, then something else will happen: *If I don't do my homework, then I will fail.* This may be sound thinking to an adult, yet from a child's perspective and considering a child's level of brain development, it simply doesn't compute. Homework needs to support children's frontal lobe development, not punish it for not being developed.

How can we continue to punish and blame our children for not being able to think clearly through homework issues when we know from scientific evidence this is a perfectly normal response? Putting stress on children to do homework after a long day of being stressed out at school is like trying to pump water from a dry well. There is nothing more to give.

The Homework. In addition to the research on the brain, research looking at the issue of homework itself is quite revealing. In fact, it is stunning. Research from the Institute of Education in the UK found that homework causes such friction between parents and children – especially in middle-class families, where concerns about a child's future can lead to a climate of pressure to succeed – that any potential educational benefits are lost.[9] Alfie Kohn, author of *The Homework Myth,* states,

> *"There is absolutely no evidence of any academic benefit from assigning homework in elementary or middle school. For younger students, in fact, there isn't even a correlation between whether children do homework (or how much they do) and any meaningful measure of achievement. At the high school level, the correlation is weak and tends to disappear when more sophisticated measures are applied. Meanwhile, no study has ever*

substantiated the belief that homework builds character or teaches good study habits."[10]

It has been shown the most effective homework is "prep," where children are asked to prepare something for an upcoming lesson. The least powerful form of homework is the most predominant form, where children are asked to finish off what they were doing in the lesson.

Emotional Regulation. When children become upset and demonstrate frustration, anger, and even hostility towards the parent or their homework, they have reached their window of stress tolerance. Or, in this case, they have reached their window of academic learning tolerance. Forcing a child through this window will result in the child losing his love for learning. It will also result in losing the opportunity to build a strong, loving, and safe relationship between the parent and child. Nothing is ever worth losing this relationship! Nothing.

Instead of creating more dysregulation for your child and being a counterforce in the connection with your child, think about becoming a positive and loving influence to the level of regulation within your child. When you resonate at a state of love, you have the power to impact your child's level of regulation. You have the power to counterbalance the dysregulation by your state of regulation.

By sitting with your child in a state of calm acceptance for the struggle he is having, you are resonating positive energy through your physiology. John Bowlby, in his work in the area of attachment theory, described how the mother is the regulator for her child. She is literally the "thermostat" to help the child shift back into a state of balance.[11]

You have witnessed this yourself. Watch a mother pick up her crying baby and with a soft voice and calm disposition, the mother is able to calm and regulate the baby. The same is true for you and your child. Your loving and calm presence, free of fear, free of expectations, and free of judgment, has the ability to shift your child's emotional state. In the late 1800's, Walt Whitman wrote about this in his poem, *Song of the Open Road*. In lines 139 and 140, he writes:

> *I and mine do not convince by arguments, similes, rhymes;*
> *We convince by our presence.*

What is exciting is that now we have the scientific evidence to back such poetic truths! In the event you do not have the same biological connection as in this example of the mother and baby (as in the case of foster or adoptive parents), regulation through your presence is still possible. It may take you digging deeper and loving deeper to bridge the gap between you and your child. Yet, this is the gift your children give to you: the gift to learn how to love with more passion, more tolerance, more openness, and more commitment. Putting love into action, even during homework times, works because love never fails.

The Traditional View proclaims, *"If your child needs you to sit with him, something is wrong."* This perspective fails to take into consideration the scientific proof that shows us children with high sensitivities to stress have difficulty self-regulating. Of course they need you to sit with them! One of the best solutions for a child who is dysregulated is to have the parent sit with him (as long as the parent can stay in a balanced state of regulation). It also takes the parent understanding and acknowledging the level of fear homework presents to the child.

For children with histories of abandonment, neglect, and rejection, facing a worksheet of homework can be like sitting down to hear a jury's verdict. It is as if this piece of paper is going to determine whether the child lives or dies. Children at this level of survival fight against doing such an assignment for hours on end. Homework time is a life-threatening event. The parent's interpretation of, *"It is only a simple sheet of math problems,"* fails to understand the dynamics and threat such a math sheet presents to the child. It takes the parent understanding and seeing what a significant threat homework can be for a child.

For the child, mistakes mean, *"I'm bad. And if I'm bad, you won't love me. And if you don't love me, I will die."* It literally comes down to such a survival-based interpretation for many children. If picking up a pencil meant that your life might be over in any second, you too would fight against doing such an assignment.

Children living at this level are unconcerned about their future. In their eyes, their future doesn't even exist. Believing these children have the capacity to even begin to *"... believe the truth, that an education is vital to their success in their adult life, and that their brain must have exercise to develop properly,"* as stated in the Traditional View, is unreasonable.

■

If picking up a pencil meant that your life might be over in any second, you too would fight against doing such an assignment.

■

They live only for the moment. Their worlds are black and white – here and now. All their resources are focused on the moment at hand to survive and ensure their safety. Long-term planning and thinking is part of the executive center of the brain's higher order-thinking, which is outside the realm of a child's primal brain activity. Expecting children to develop and engage in this type of thinking comes from an adult perspective, void of any understanding of the child's level of survival thinking.

Solutions. While the best solution would be to place a cease and desist order on homework altogether, this may not be possible. Here is a list of solutions that work to decrease stress around homework which simultaneously works to help a child learn to regulate during these stressful times:

1. **Have your child teach you what he is learning in school.** Those who teach are the greatest students. When you take interest in your child's schoolwork, you are giving him the message that what he is learning is important. This is also an opportunity to join your child in his world, an opportunity lost far too often. When parents jump into a child's world, the child feels important, special, and loved. These then correlate to building a strong foundation with the child, creating a secure attachment with the child.

2. **Focus on helping your child regulate during difficult moments.** Teach your children how to take deep breaths to calm their neurological systems. Interrupt negative feedback loops by taking breaks with them. Go for a walk, play with the family dog, or have a snack together. Keep in mind that none of their resistance is intentional. It isn't against you. It is an internal battle going on within your child's heart – it is a manifestation of self-rejection. Sometimes this self-rejection rears its ugly head against you, the parent, because it feels better for the child than feeling the self-rejection he has for himself.

3. **Break down the assignment into pieces.** Understand your child is feeling so overwhelmed that he cannot do the work. It is not that he won't; he simply can't. Relate this to your own experiences of being overwhelmed in your work.

You walk into the office and see you have 150 e-mails to answer, the voicemail is flashing indicating you have numerous calls to return, your inbox is overflowing, and your boss just stopped by to remind you an extensive report is due at noon. How do you feel? What do you do to overcome this feeling? Maybe you get up and go to the break room and get some coffee (a regulatory beverage).

So for your child, break up the 20 spelling words and start with just five. Yes, just five. Five is better than none. Five is better than pencils being broken or paper being shredded. Work to build up your child's window of homework tolerance. Eventually he will be able to do 10, then 15, and then 20. Trust in the process and stop pushing your child well beyond his capabilities.

Remember you had to learn to walk before you could run. For children to find their way through homework assignments, we must realize it is a sequential process. Baby steps now will lead to giant leaps in the future.

4. **Allow children to have a voice about their homework and give them emotional space.** Children have not learned to use their voice or they haven't been given permission to use their voice. Instead, they fight and rebel against the assignments. We as parents, in fear our children won't pass or, worse, that we will look like bad parents because our child is not completing his homework, fight back with controlling measures to save face with the teacher.

It takes the parent shifting out of her own fear and stepping into the child's fear. The fight your child is putting on is saying, *"I can't do this anymore. Stop controlling me and stop making me do this because it is only making me worse!"* How would you feel if your boss pushed you and pushed you and fought you over getting an assignment completed? Think about how it would feel to be controlled like this. You would fight back or simply quit! It is no different for your child.

Trying to convince your child he needs to do his homework will only breed more resistance. Giving him logical reasons as to why he needs to care about his homework and his education will leave him feeling isolated and on his own to defend his position. Your child needs you to listen to him before he can listen to you. Here is an example of an interaction that helped Michael get through his resistance to homework:

Mom: *"Let's look at today's schedule and you tell me what time you would like to do your homework."*

Michael: *"I don't care about any schedule because I'm not doing my homework."*

Mom: *"Wow. You sound like you're quite upset, Michael."*

Michael: *"Of course I'm upset. I hate doing homework!"*

Mom: *"I can see that."*

Michael: *"Why do I have to spend my playtime doing homework? I'm at school all day long."*

Mom: *"That is hard, isn't it?"*

Michael: *"I hate it. And you can't make me do it. I don't care if I fail."*

Mom: *"That's how hard it is for you, isn't it?*

Michael: *"I'm sick of it all."*

Mom: *"It's hard doing all of this on your own, isn't it Michael?"*

Michael: *(Nodding his head to say, "Yes, it is!")*

Mom: *"What can I do to help you, sweetheart?"*

Michael: *"I don't know."*

Mom: *"Maybe I can sit down with you and help you, just today?"*

Michael: *"Maybe."*

Mom: *"This is too much to have to handle on your own. I'm here to help you through it."*

Michael: *"Okay."*

Children simply need support and validation from their parents. They do have the ability to make good choices. They need to know they are understood and supported, not judged and controlled. It takes the power of the parent-child relationship to help shift them into the right direction. They do have it within them.

5. **Reduce all stress-inducing factors surrounding homework.** Eliminate any stressors in the home environment that might be stress inducing and creating more overwhelm for your child. Additionally, see if there are any factors at school creating more stress around homework for your child. Many times just the thought of a consequence for not finishing homework, such as not being able to go to recess or being singled out from the other students, is enough to create such a black cloud around a child that his level of stress becomes completely overwhelming and stifles any ability he may have to complete the work. Ironically, consequences intended to motivate become the block that decreases or entirely stifles motivation.

> ■
>
> *Ironically, consequences intended to create and motivate become the block that decrease or entirely stifle motivation.*
>
> ■

In such a case, speak with the child's teacher and explain that your child has a high sensitivity to stress and the fear-driven consequence is creating a negative situation for your child. Some teachers resist adjusting their policies for one student, saying, "If I make an exception for this child, I'll have to make an exception for every child." The reality is that not every child is having this difficulty and needs this exception. Meeting the needs of one child to ensure a successful educational experience should always be the priority.

6. **Find different times of the day to complete the homework.** Allow time after coming home from school for your child to reconnect with you instead of insisting he complete his homework right away. Yes, it would make life easier just to have it done and not have to worry about it for the rest of the evening. However, the reality is your child may not be able to do this.

Relate this to your own experiences. When you get off work, do you feel like pulling out your briefcase and sitting down to do more work? Or if you are a stay-at-home parent, when you finish cooking the last meal of the day, do you feel like spending the next hour or two in the kitchen drumming up a new recipe? No. You are depleted of your internal sense of motivation and drained of any creativity at this point. You need to be refueled. The same is true for your child.

Have your child set what time of the evening he would like to come back to finish the homework. Work with him to help him learn how to schedule his afternoon. If your child continues to struggle in the evenings with completing the homework, ask the teacher for the flexibility to complete the homework on the weekends. Weekends are less stressful and the relaxed atmosphere can create a drastically different environment for your child to find his way through the stress of homework.

7. **Reduce the pressure you place on your child to complete the homework.** Your expectations need to be equivalent to the emotional readiness of your child. If you came from a home environment where academics were paramount to success, examine these beliefs objectively to determine if you are putting this past family stress on your child.

Accept that your child is doing the best he can do for this moment. Trust that he has the capacity to do more and know without a doubt that time will come. It takes meeting your child where he is to help him develop a stronger self-regulatory system and to find his own internal sense of motivation. Forcing and threatening will only block progress and create resentment towards you and his entire educational career.

8. **Work through the homework problems with your child.** Children can learn by demonstration as well as by doing the work themselves. If your child is resisting doing the work by himself, do it with him. In fact, if his fear drives so much resistance to the homework process, complete the homework for him. Yes. You read that correctly. Do it *for* him. Simply ask your child to sit with you and talk through the problem as you complete it.

This may challenge your values and belief system to the core and that is good because this means you are opening up to the truth about homework. Homework is intended to help children, not hurt them. By going as far as doing the work for him, he is still learning. He is learning the academic material by your teaching. Yes, I hear your fear saying, *"No, what my child will learn is how to manipulate his mother into doing his homework for him."* This is the fear that keeps us from making homework time different. Trust in the process. We simply need to slow down and allow the negative neurological feedback loop (refer to *Beyond Consequences, Logic, and Control*, Volume 1) around homework to be interrupted. By doing the homework for him, you are creating a positive homework experience free of stress and threat. Your child will learn the important fact that you are committed to helping him and you will take every step possible to ensure his success. This is the ultimate lesson in learning responsibility – having someone take responsibility for you teaches you how to take responsibility in the future.

Within a short time, you will find your child actually wants to do the homework himself instead of you doing it. Children do not like sitting and watching. They are doers. They like to participate; they do not like to be bystanders. How many children do you see sitting on a park bench just watching the other children play? None. They want to do it. Give your child the jump-start to doing his homework and help him break the barrier he has been fighting to maintain for protection. Make it safe. Make it fun. Create joy in stressful situations. That is a gift your child will then be able to take into any "real life" situation as he becomes an adult.

The bottom line is that low stress environments keep the brain calm and regulated. The people in this environment, the intensity of requirements and expectations, and the level of emotional openness will influence the effectiveness of this environment for children required to do homework. In the past, too much emphasis has been placed on getting children to complete the work without consideration of any of these factors.

Creating negative experiences around education and learning for our children is a tragedy. No homework assignment is EVER worth sacrificing a child's self-worth or suffocating a child's natural desire to explore and learn. When approaching the task of homework, stay focused on helping your child move forward, not backwards in his educational career. Stay attuned to both your regulation and your child's level of regulation. And most of all, when fear overcomes love in the connection between you and your child, homework time is officially over for the day.

Parenting Example: Homework

Scenario: Danny, an 8-year-old, was continually having trouble with his math homework. His teacher would give him a packet at the first of the week to be turned in on Fridays. When he did work on the math, it appeared Danny was intentionally doing the problems wrong. An assignment that should have taken less than 15 minutes would take all night or he would save it for the next day and let the work build up until it was due.

Traditional View

His mother knows that Danny HAS to do his homework and that he MUST get it completed. There are no other options. Certainly he can add 4+6 by now and not come up with 46! This is clearly a passive aggressive way of him refusing to do his homework.

His mother makes it clear to Danny there is not going to be a way out of the homework and it will need to be completed (without ridiculous answers). Danny is matter-of-factly given the rule that "chores and homework come first, playing second."[11] When Danny wants to meet his friends to play basketball and his homework is not done, this will teach an important lesson in good work habits and responsibility.

Danny's mother is responsible for the house and doing the things Danny can't do on his own. Homework is not her responsibility...it is Danny's. She understands if she interferes in any way with the homework, she will only be enabling him to resist more. This is a life lesson that has be taught now. Additionally, his report card is a measure of his progress, not his mother's. If Danny fails, it is simply a natural consequence for him to finally wake-up and embrace his reality.

A New View

Danny's mom realizes this is not how life is suppose to be. She goes to him, sits with him, and says, *"I love you more than math, Danny. I want to be able to make homework time different for us. How about I sit with you today and be here with you?"* She knew it would take a tremendous amount of her effort to show him she really did love him more than math, considering all the negative experiences they had in the past.

For the first two weeks of trying this approach, Danny regressed and demanded mom's attention for each and every problem. He would go as far as not even being able to count. Mom simply gave him understanding, along with the answers to the problems. Even when his mom gave him the answers, he would write down the wrong answer!

By the end of the second week, Danny began to complete some of the work on his own but then would suddenly pull back, as if to check and make sure his mom was still there to support him. Mom continued to flow with Danny and meet his needs. She now understood this was not about manipulation but about a child who needed reassurance and security.

A few months later, Danny's mom writes, *"I am able to pull back more from his school work and let him work independently. His behaviors have improved greatly. I know that if he is seeking my attention, he MUST need it. So, I give him my attention even when I know he is capable because when he is dysregulated, he slips back. I sit at the table with him during these times but never for as long as I had to before. I simply sit with him long enough for him to know I love him more than math. He ends his math now feeling very pleased with himself. His outlook on life and his feeling of self-worth are so much better."*

True story!

Quick Reference
Homework

Remember that a child resisting homework:
- Is in a state of overwhelm.
- Is in a state of confused thinking and literally may not be able to add or read.
- Does not need you to remove privileges, give consequences, or use any other fear-based tactic to motivate him. These will only create more stress and increase his overwhelm.
- Is feeling threatened and may feel as if he doesn't perform he will not be loved.
- Perceives the homework as a life-threatening event.
- Is not being defiant from a control perspective. He is simply working to protect himself.

When helping a child struggling with homework, recognize he needs you to:
- Simply be present with him and help him regulate so he can find his internal calmness.
- Reassure him with unconditional love so his security is not based on his performance.
- Put him in the driver's seat. Have him teach you what he is learning.
- Break down assignments into manageable pieces.
- Give him emotional space to voice his opinion about homework without working to convince him why he needs to do homework.
- Reduce all peripheral factors that might be contributing to additional stress around homework.
- Be flexible in the times of day he does his homework.
- Reduce the pressure you place on him.
- Work through homework problems with him, even do them for him at first.
- Love him more than math, more than reading – more than any homework assignment.
- Trust in the process!

CHAPTER THIRTEEN

Chores

■

*"At worst, a house unkept cannot
be so distressing as a life unlived."*
– Rose Macaulay

Chores. Think about this little word, chores. Say the word in your head to yourself. What physiological response surfaces? Maybe you feel your face scrunching up, perhaps your stomach turns into a knot, or maybe your shoulders tighten up. Now say the word out loud: CHORES. Listen to your tone of voice when you say it. Look into the mirror and watch your facial expression. Are your eyes rolling? Is your head shaking? For many people, you might as well be saying, ROOT CANAL.

The word "chores" is a loaded word, which begs us to stop and ask two basic questions: **"How has this word developed so much negativity around it?"** and **"What interactions have transpired between parents and children to create this?"**

To start, the word itself has a negative definition. The Merriam Webster dictionary defines chore as "a difficult or disagreeable task." When we define something as difficult or disagreeable from the beginning, we are creating something difficult and disagreeable! Whoever decided to call them chores to begin with?

If you Google the word "chores," you will find an amazing number of articles written on this subject. Articles in monthly parenting magazines are filled with the topic of getting children to finish their chores. Look through the index of parenting books and you'll find pages devoted to the topic of chores. All of these sources offer basically the same information centered on getting the child to complete the chore. These resources offer the same techniques...they are simply repackaging the same information over and over, with different titles and different authors. If we keep repeating this information yet the demand for solutions continues, could it be that the information being offered is ineffective?

As will be shown in this chapter, these traditional approaches are ineffective because somewhere along the way, the focus of getting the chore completed took precedence above all else. In these traditional outcome focused approaches, the importance of the parent-child relationship disintegrated. Balance between the two was lost...the completion of the chore dominated the family, despite the negativity and disconnect that resulted. Control took over. Winning the power struggle became more important than the emotional wellness of family members. In short, **fear won out over love** when it came to completing chores.

Traditional View

Traditionally, chores have been viewed as an absolute necessity for children to learn to be responsible. Chores have been viewed as a way to teach children that being part of a family means giving back to the family. Countless parenting books all come to this one conclusion: "Children need a certain amount of responsibility and need to learn to be accountable for their actions." The Traditional View states that parents need to require their children, as young as 2 and 3 years old, to do household chores to help them be more well rounded, organized, and responsible as they grow.

To ensure this goal, traditional parenting offers a plethora of ways to get children to do their chores. Chore charts placed on the refrigerator are recommended. When children accomplish their chores, they receive a sticker. After a certain number of stickers, the child gets a reward such as a toy, a trip to the movies, or a new book. Using positive reinforcement to solve children's issues has been recommended by child behavior experts, including the American Academy of Pediatrics. The American Academy of Pediatrics also recommends "applying punishment to reduce or eliminate undesired behaviors."[1]

Parenting experts declare children are "just lazy by nature"[2] and warn if parents "set the precedent of always reminding and coaxing children, then they will always be reminding and coaxing."[3] The warning stresses that you as a parent, are not running a hotel but a home.

For attachment-challenged children, chores have traditionally been used as a method of discipline. Several attachment experts recommend instead of using timeouts, parents should use chores.[4] The use of chores is seen as a way to help children "heal" and earn their way into the family. One parenting advisor states children should do about 30 minutes of chores each day for a minimum of six days a week. Playtime and mealtime are given only after the chore is completed.[5] The thought with this approach is that this is how to get children to give, by helping the family. The requirement is also that the child do the chore "fast, snappy, and right."[6] The parent is in charge of making certain the chore is done to the parent's standard. If a child refuses to do the chore, "he needs to sit and rest until he gets over it."

Other attachment specialists use chores as a way to stay ahead of attachment disordered children. The use of chores removes the child's sense of control, giving full control to the parent in order for the child to release his need to control his life. By releasing this control, the child is depending on his parent and attachment can then begin. Additionally, other specialists state that chores used as a consequence build conscience and social empathy.[7]

A New View

The traditional literature is focused on the need to teach or heal children through the use of chores. From a parental perspective, this may be perfectly sound thinking; yet from a child's perspective, we need to examine the validity of this approach. It is time to consider the outcome of what has traditionally happened in homes to get children to finish their chores. We need to be willing to observe with an open mind and with consideration of what has happened to our children from a relational level due to this mindset.

The reality is this: **What has happened far too often in the quest to teach children responsibility through completing their chores has taught them how easily their family can switch from stability to chaos, negativity, and turmoil.** We have used controlling actions around chores, which have then created negative repetitious experiences around doing housework. This negativity has bred resentment (both in the parents and the children). This resentment has bred disconnect. And this disconnect has contributed to a lack of loving and fulfilling relationships between parents and their children.

It is time to change and realize that nothing is ever worth losing the quality of family life and the parent-child relationship, not even chores. Consider these questions:

(1) "Is a clean room really worth a disconnected relationship with my child?"
(2) "Is a swept floor worth my child seeing me as the enemy and him as the victim?"
(3) "Is forcing my child to take responsibility actually teaching him anything about taking responsibility or am I teaching him how to grow up and control people?"

Perhaps you are feeling disrespected. After all, you drive them to school, to football practice, cook them dinner, etc. The least they could do is simply put their laundry away! Yet what we need to recognize is many children are too dysregulated to get outside of themselves and give back to the family. To move to this state of giving, which comes from an internal place of motivation, it is essential they become secure in themselves and their existence as an important part of the family. If they are not secure or calm internally, reaching beyond who they are, out of a place of survival, is impossible. It is simply outside their scope of human nature.

The Parent's Own Self-Understanding. Our own fears as parents of raising children who are selfish, who do not contribute, or who are lazy, can keep us focused only on getting the chore completed, with no consideration of what is happening beyond this immediate goal. We can easily lose sight of how our fears affect the negative neurological feedback loops (see *Beyond Consequences, Logic, and Control,* Volume 1). Old messages from the past are often part of the stress we as parents unknowingly bring into the chore equation. New messages from traditional parenting experts, based from a negative perspective of the child, create more of these parental fears. When parents are told children are just lazy, parents easily position themselves on the defense against their child to make certain they win the lazy versus responsible child battle to be successful parents. Such interpretations of the child's behaviors give no attention to the emotional needs of the child or the parent.

When first addressing how to change the chores pattern in your household, it is important to be willing to look honestly into your own fears, a concept completely absent from the traditional perspective. What are some of the old messages driving your intensity or your rigidity around your child completing his chores? Could these messages include any of the following?

1. "Cleanliness is next to godliness."
2. "If my house is clean, I am a good parent."
3. "Sally works full-time and her house is immaculate. What is wrong with me? I'm home all day and my house is a mess!"
4. "I can get my staff of 50 people to follow my directives, yet my child won't even pick up after himself after I've told him a thousand times!"

The responsibility to make changes in the house starts first with the parent's own self-understanding. Explore what it means for you to have your child complete his chores. Explore what the interpretation is for you, as a parent, when your child follows through and follows your directives. More importantly, what are the negative messages tied to your child NOT completing his chores? These negative messages may have strong emotional consequences, driving you and intensifying your reactions to your child. These negative messages need to be acknowledged and understood before you can expect significant changes from your children around the issue of chores.

Five Critical Success Factors. Once you have been honest with your own fears and needs, the next step is to a look at five key points regarding chores. When reviewing the traditional parenting literature regarding chores, it becomes clear these factors have been missing. These include:

1. Children are emotional beings and when we fail to meet them at this level, even simple chores like taking out the garbage become monumental obstacles.
2. Children are children and they do not have an inherent need to pick up after themselves.
3. The use of external motivators (chore charts, consequences, etc.) stifles the development of a child's natural internal cooperative spirit.
4. The parent's expectation of the chore must coincide with the child's developmental and emotional age, not the child's chronological age.
5. We have missed valuable opportunities to engage with our children and strengthen our relationship in our quest to have chores accomplished.

Understanding these five factors is critical to the success of families alleviating issues around chores – so critical, in fact, that I am calling them the "Five Critical Success Factors." Once these are acknowledged, understood, and applied, you will be able to make significant changes in your family – chores won't be such a chore anymore.

Critical Success Factor 1:

Children are emotional beings and when we fail to meet them at this level, even simple chores like taking out the garbage become monumental obstacles.

The traditional model of working with children to complete their chores is void in the area of meeting a child's emotional needs. Children's emotional needs are not only ignored but are not even acknowledged in most traditional models. Parenting books and articles regarding chores speak nothing to the emotional needs of the child. They speak only to the cognitive and rational thought process of the adults.

This is reflective of living in an "emotionally phobic" society. As a culture, emotions are scary and uncomfortable. We have found refuge and safety in intellect. As adults, we live our lives from this intellectual, cognitive, and rational framework. Many of us did not have our own emotional needs met as children, so the only way we could connect with our parents was to shift out of our original emotional framework into an adult cognitive framework.

Children with difficult behaviors give us the gift of returning back to this emotional framework. These children are often so stressed and overwhelmed that they are "stuck" in this emotional place. The only way to help them is to jump into that space with them. This does not require extensive therapy. It can happen in the daily activities of life – chore time is a perfect opportunity! Instead of intellectualizing the need to do chores, we need, just for a few moments, to join our children in this place of emotional dysregulation. An example of "how" to do this is included in the next section.

Critical Success Factor 2:

Children are children and they do not have an inherent need to pick up after themselves.

Children live in the moment. Their worlds are about them. There is little internal motivation; they cannot see any value in doing chores, especially children in survival mode. The idea of a dirty room being unacceptable simply does not register in a child's mind. That is an adult interpretation.

Traditional parenting techniques have used external rewards to compensate for this lack of internal motivation. While for many children this system has been effective, for children with traumatic histories, whose foundation of security and safety is unstable, the use of these external motivators is completely ineffective. Here is a question posed by one parent of a child with a trauma history: "We are using a rewards chart for chores and it is absolutely not working. Any suggestions?"

The suggestion would be to realize we have a child with no internal need to do chores combined with a child who has a high sensitivity to stress. Reward charts can be too overwhelming for some children and simply stress them to a higher degree, pushing them well beyond their window of stress tolerance.

Instead, parents can focus on the relationship and give the child emotional space to have a voice about not wanting to do the chore. When children feel heard and understood, they are more apt to do what the parent has requested, even if they don't see a need or flat out disagree with the request. Here is one father's story with his 9-year-old son. Notice how he was able to implement both Critical Success Factors 1 and 2:

> One Saturday I walked into my son's room to announce the agenda for the morning: "Daniel, it is time to rake the leaves so I can mow the lawn this morning." Daniel kept playing and simply ignored my request. Instead of threatening him with no more toys or reminding him his chore would earn him five points on his point chart, I stopped and recognized this approach never worked in previous weeks. I finally realized Daniel was involved in his play. Given the chance to play or rake leaves, which would I choose? Well, of course I would choose to play. Most importantly, I realized he had no concept that I needed those leaves raked to get everything completed on my list of things to do that Saturday, so I went and sat next to him.
>
> "Daniel, you really don't want to rake those leaves do you?" Continuing to play, he shook his head "no." I said to him in an empathetic tone, "I'm not going to try to convince you why I need those leaves raked because I really understand that raking those leaves means nothing to you." Daniel replied, "It's just stupid! The minute I get done, that tree just drops more leaves and then I have to just do it again!" Instead of providing reasoning and logic, I replied, "That is frustrating, isn't it?" Raising the volume and tone of his voice, Daniel immediately fired back, "It's stupid! I hate raking them." I had to admit to myself, it is somewhat of a

repetitive job. "I know, son. It just isn't very much fun. I have a hard time doing some of the chores I have to do, also. I mow the lawn and then, bam, it grows back and I have to mow it again the next week!" I allowed Daniel space to relate my experience to his and I just sat with him for a few minutes. Then, I offered to help get him started, "How about I get the rake and garbage bags ready while you get to a stopping point with your toys. Just leave them there and they'll be right here when you get done with the raking. You'll be able to pick back up right where you left off." I said this to reassure him that nothing he has now will be taken away, working to give him security of what he has in the present will still be there in the future.

I went outside and started getting everything ready for Daniel. In less than three minutes, he was actually out there with me, getting the leaves done so he could return to his play. Success!

Critical Success Factor 3:

The use of external motivators (chore charts, consequences, etc.) stifles the development of a child's natural internal cooperative spirit.

Children *do* have a need to make their parents happy and there is an internal cooperative spirit deep within them. **There is no other person on this planet they want to please more.** Don't we as adults still seek our parents' approval, even if they have passed away?

Children with attachment challenges and difficult behaviors may act as though they do not want to please their parents, and many traditional attachment therapists will state that until there is an attachment, the child will not want to please the parent. However, we are biologically designed to be in relationship. This is actually more of a necessity for a child with a traumatic history. These children are feeling unsafe in what appears to them as a threatening world. A relationship would actually ensure their survival and from a primal level, they know that is what they need the most! Yet, their experiences are telling them relationships are dangerous, so their behaviors are simply demonstrating they are terrified to be in a parent-child relationship. What a place of discomfort for a child to live – two opposing forces – one seeking relationships, the other seeking disconnect, yet both with the goal of safety and security.

To help our children find their way through this fear and out of survival, it takes giving them an environment of feeling safe. This will help them uncover their intrinsic cooperative spirit from within. Putting surface rewards and superficial prizes in front of them only creates more overwhelm. Using external rewards leaves them on their own to navigate their dysregulation and fear.

This is the biggest irony of all – **we have been trying to teach children to cooperate but we have not been cooperating with them in their efforts to manage their pain and overwhelm.** The very thing we have been trying to teach, we have not been modeling for them. Children learn by modeling, not through commands and directives from people in charge of them.

Critical Success Factor 4:

The parent's expectation of the chores needs to coincide with the child's developmental and emotional age, not the child's chronological age.

Children with traumatic histories typically operate at a much younger emotional and developmental age than their actual chronological age. This means you may have a 9-year-old who is more like a 5-year-old. If your 9-year-old's chore is to wash the car, that would be like asking a 5-year-old to wash your car. This would be outside his developmental capacity.

When we can see this from the child's emotional and developmental perspective, we can see the resistance to doing the chore is often simply reflecting his lack of ability and his feeling of being overwhelmed, rather than a matter of disobedience and defiance. For example, let us suppose your position at work is to complete the budget for your department of six employees. Your boss walks in and asks you to complete the budget not only for your department but for the entire company of 500 employees. How would you feel – overwhelmed and at a loss?

Take a step back and truly consider if the tasks you are asking your child to accomplish are too much. If your child has been consistently resistant, this is a communication that it is too much. What is your child's developmental age and do the chores match this age? Simply readjusting what is expected of your child can lower your child's stress level. Table 1 lists some suggested age-appropriate chores for children. This is a general list to give you an idea of what chores would be appropriate according to your child's age. View it from your child's emotional and developmental age, not his chronological age.

Table 1

Developmental Age	Suggested Chores
Ages 4 to 5	• Put toys away. • Fill pet's food dish. • Put clothes in hamper. • Wipe up spills. • Dust.
Ages 6 to 7	• Make own bed. • Sort laundry. • Empty wastebaskets. • Bring in mail or newspaper. • Pick up crumbs with hand-held vacuum. • Water flowers. • Unload utensils from dishwasher. • Wash plastic dishes at sink. • Fix bowl of ccreal. • Weed and rake leaves.
Ages 8 to 9	• Wash table after meals. • Take out garbage. • Put away own laundry. • Set and clear table. • Help make and pack lunch. • Keep bedroom tidy. • Pour own drinks. • Answer telephone. • Make own snacks.
Ages 10 to 11	• Load dishwasher. • Fold laundry. • Put away groceries. • Vacuum. • Wash car. • Help make dinner. • Make own breakfast. • Cook simple foods. • Sweep floors. • Take pet for a walk. • Sew buttons.
Ages 12 +	• Unload dishwasher. • Clean bathroom. • Wash windows. • Cook simple meal with supervision. • Do laundry. • Baby-sit younger siblings • Mow lawn. • Clean kitchen. • Change bed. • Make cookies or cake from a box mix.

Critical Success Factor 5:

We have missed valuable opportunities to engage with our children and strengthen our relationship in our quest to have chores accomplished.

In the quest to get our children to do their chores, all too often we have missed valuable opportunities to connect with our children. We work to plan fun activities like going to the park or going swimming, yet some of the simplest activities of our daily lives have created chaos instead of fun and connection.

When a child is dysregulated – being defiant about doing his chores – this is an opportune time to connect with him. In fact, it isn't just an opportune time, it is an essential time to connect with him. Unfortunately, traditional parenting advises just the opposite. It encourages parents to stick to the directive and hold rigid boundaries to "win" the chores battle.

Dr. Allan Shore, considered the "American Bowlby," combines recent scientific research with the foundation of attachment theory from John Bowlby. He states that attachment is about joy. It is about "joining the child." The attachment relationship is comprised of "enjoyment, joy, interest, and excitement." He states when the parent and child are connected, their bodily systems are being activated and they are co-regulating. These two bodily systems are linked together by their autonomic nervous systems. [8]

Applying this knowledge to children and families, namely chores, would it not be more productive to "join" our children when they are dysregulated? By joining them, we would be linking with their bodily system, making the experience of doing a "chore" less of a chore and creating a time of connection and regulation. It would be an opportunity for enjoyment, joy, interest, and excitement. Here is a mother who tells her story about her teenage sons:

> *My two sons (actually they are my nephews) came to live with me two years ago. They are now 14 and 16 years old. Since coming to live with me, their behaviors have been beyond comprehensible. Not only is there an amazing amount of defiance and disrespect, but they have been literally tearing my house apart. Walls have holes in them, doors are off the hinges – it looks like a war zone. I have asked them to do just one chore and that*

has been to simply take out the garbage. I have been met with total resistance every time. Finally, I began to understand this fifth point about joining the child in his overwhelm. After asking Jimmy to take out the garbage, I added, "I'll go with you if you would like." Well, the truth is, he still resisted. So, I said to him, "That is okay, how about I do it this time and we'll work on making it different next time." I did this every night for four nights in a row. By the fifth night, Jimmy actually came with me! I couldn't believe it. We had a chance to connect and I worked hard to keep myself regulated and in check, being mindful of not saying what first came to my mind, "Well, it is about time!" Instead, I stayed present with him in that moment and told him I was glad to be able to have some time with him. One evening we stayed on the back porch after taking out the garbage and had a great conversation together. This was something we had not been able to have in a few months. To conclude this chore story with an amazing outcome, by two weeks later, Jimmy was taking the garbage out by himself! Two weeks is all it took. I had been fighting this for the past two years and was able to turn it all around in a short two weeks! This stuff really works.

It can be this simple when you shift your perspective, understand, and address the emotional and developmental issues surrounding the completion of chores, both from your perspective as a parent and from your child's perspective. The examples in this chapter, and in all the chapters of this book, are all true testimonies given by parents who were able to simply change how they saw their child's resistance to doing chores as well as understand their reactions to their child. I cannot emphasize enough and encourage you enough to view chores as an opportunity for connection, not as a challenge of strife, power, and control. It might be extreme, but the next time your child says, *"What? Take out the garbage? Do I have to?"* I want you to celebrate the moment in front of you! This is the moment to teach, connect, and end the negative cycling that has developed from taking the traditional approach. Have fun with chores instead of making them a difficult or tedious undertaking.

> ■
>
> *View chores as an opportunity for connection, not as a challenge of strife, power, and control.*
>
> ■

Parenting Example: Chores

Scenario:

Adam, 9 years old, had been asked to clean up his room every day for the past week. Saturday was given as the absolute deadline that the room had to be cleaned. Instead of cleaning his room during the week to keep the mess to a minimum, Adam's room was an absolute bomb by Saturday.

Traditional View

Mom: *"Adam, it's Saturday. Time to do your chores. You need to clean up your bedroom."*

Adam: Ignores Mom's request and continues playing.

Mom: *"Adam, are you listening to me? I told you to clean your room."*

Adam: Continues to ignore Mom. Mom gets busy doing something else and forgets about it for a while.

Mom: (frustrated now) *"Haven't you cleaned your room yet Adam? I told you to do that half an hour ago and you haven't even started on it yet."*

Adam: Ignores Mom again.

Mom: *"Adam, don't pretend you can't hear me. Just get up and start cleaning your room."*

Adam: Continues to ignore Mom.

Mom: (really frustrated now). *"You know you always have to clean your room on Saturday. It's not like you've never had to do it before. If you had started when I told you to in the first place it would be almost finished by now. You always make life so hard for yourself."*

Adam: *"I don't want to. I want you to help me."*

Mom: *"Why should I? You made the mess. I've been telling you all week to clean it up. If you had listened to me then, there wouldn't be so much mess to clean up now. I'm busy cleaning the rest of the house and doing the laundry and sorting out the shopping. You don't seem very interested in helping me with all those chores. All I'm asking you to do is clean up your own mess. It's not that hard."*

Adam: *"But I want you to help me."*

Mom: *"No, now you're starting to make me really cross. Why*

do we have to go through this every single week?" Mom
slips into a sarcastic mode and becomes the narrator of
their situation. *"It's always the same. Adam refuses to clean
his room. Mom gets completely stressed out and angry.
She makes Adam sit in his room till he cleans it. He stays
in there for two hours and still doesn't end up cleaning
anything. Mom remains stressed the rest of the day. Adam
remains stressed the rest of the day and the room remains
uncleaned."* Switching back to speaking to Adam directly,
*"Well, it is up to you. This is your responsibility and you're
going to have to learn to participate in cleaning your part
of the house. It is up to you if you want to make it difficult
or not."*

A New View

Mom: Notices that the room has been getting messier and messier
all week, but also recognizes they all have been too busy to
do anything about it. *"Okay, Adam, I think it's about time
we got in and sorted your room out a bit. We can hardly get
in the door!"*

Adam: *"But I'm busy playing now. I don't want to do it now. I'll do
it later."*

Mom: *"We're going out later, and we won't be able to do it then, so
now would be a good time to do it."*

Adam: *"But I don't want to. I want to play."*

Mom: *"I can see you're really enjoying what you're doing now. I
know it's hard to stop playing when you're having so much
fun."*

Adam: *"But I want you to help me clean it."*

Mom: Mom knows that she wants to change the pattern that has
continued week after week and realizes the room is overwhelming even for her. *"Sure. I'll help you. I know when your
bedroom gets that messy it can seem really daunting and
overwhelming. It's hard to know where to start, isn't it?"*

Adam: *"Yes, there's so much mess I don't know how to clean it all."*

Mom: *"That's okay sweetheart. We'll do it together. You start over
there and just pick up all the Lego bits first."*

Mom:	Mom starts packing stuff away and Adam packs away his Legos. *"Great work, Adam. Now, can you pick up the dirty clothes and put them in the laundry basket for me?"*
Mom:	They continue cleaning the room together and get it all done. *"That's great Adam. Look at your room now. Doesn't it look great and feel great? Now you can find your toys when you want them. We still have time before we have to go out, so you can keep playing if you would like."*
Adam:	*"Thanks for helping me Mom. I just didn't know where to start. There was so much mess."*
Mom:	*"That's okay, Adam. I'll always be here to help you. I love you."*
Adam:	*"I love you too, Mom."*

True story!

Quick Reference
Chores

Remember that a child resistant to chores is:
- A child who does not have an inherent need for chores.
- In need of you meeting him emotionally, not intellectually.
- Better motivated through a strong relationship rather than through external rewards in the long term.
- Possibly being asked to do chores beyond his emotional and developmental capabilities.
- A child who needs connection, not consequences.

When helping a child to do his chores, recognize he needs you to:
- Take responsibility for your own fears and your own reactions.
- Keep the perspective that no chore is worth shifting from stability to chaos.
- Focus on your relationship with him and give him emotional space to have a voice.
- Help him regulate to shift from a state of overwhelm into a state of calm.
- Trust there is no other person on this planet he wants to please more.
- Cooperate with him so he can learn how to cooperate with you.
- Evaluate if the chore is too extreme in regards to his emotional age.
- Take this resistance and turn it into an opportunity for connection, love, and relationship building.
- Join him in working through this difficult moment to give him a positive experience around chores.
- Make chores less of a chore.

PART THREE

Parenting Bonus Section

CHAPTER FOURTEEN

Real-Life Stories from Real-Life Parents with Real-Life Children

■

Since the release of *Beyond Consequences, Logic, and Control*¸ Volume 1, I have received incredible testimonials from parents around the world who have been able to make major shifts in their families with this parenting model. These parents submitted these stories especially for you to read in this Volume 2. They wanted to share the life-changing moments they were able to create with their children, simply by putting love into action. As I was reading them when they first arrived in my email inbox, tears of joy and amazement filled my heart. I hope they touch you as much as they did me.

I wish I had known about your work years ago. In fact, I wish I had gotten your book three weeks ago. Instead, I gave up.

I had ordered your book, *Beyond Consequences, Logic, and Control*. I didn't wait for it to arrive. I didn't think things could get better...and I couldn't stand how bad things had gotten. My husband and daughter were screaming. I snapped. I grabbed a bottle of Xanax and some wine and headed out. I ended up in intensive care in the hospital for five days. Sheer good fortune and no cars on the road prevented a more tragic outcome. I was incredibly stupid.

I didn't intend to end my life when I took the pills. I had no idea how strong they were. I just wanted the stress and unhappiness to end...for at least a few minutes.

Skip forward to Christmas Eve. I returned home from the hospital. I felt worse than ever. Our finances were in even worse shape than before. My husband was so traumatized he had to take leave from work. My daughter didn't seem to care that I was safe. My son called but didn't come over. He lives less than 10 minutes from our house. I was glad to be out of the hospital but I still didn't feel hopeful about the future. I glanced at the mail and saw a large envelope. It had your book. I thought to myself, "Another waste of money. Why in the world did I buy that? These kids will never love us."

I was wrong. It's only been 10 days and already our family dynamics are improving. Things with our daughter are the most peaceful they have ever been. Considering she has been in and out of residential treatment centers and hospitals for four years, that's an incredible statement. It's probably too late to heal the Great Divide with our son because he joined the military and leaves for boot camp next month. We rarely see him and he responds with intense rage at the slightest disagreement. However, I don't feel the profound sense of hopelessness I had before. My husband and I feel we have at least a chance to connect with our 18-year-old daughter.

Last night was a good test. Liana flipped out over a minor thing. She lost something she needed and was having a panic attack. I didn't try to fix it. I just kept sending her loving, peaceful thoughts. She attacked me verbally but I didn't overreact. I responded gently and courteously. She stormed off and I let things cool off. I felt a sense of peace that this was going to turn out differently and not escalate into a huge meltdown.

I went in later to see her and told her if she had any questions, I would be glad to help. She took a deep breath and had a sigh of relief. Then I asked if she wanted to watch the TV show, *Ugly Betty,* with me. She laughed and then even apologized. Today, she found what she was looking for and gave me big hugs and thanks for being there for her. What a turnaround.

Like I said earlier, I wish we had known about your work years ago...or three weeks ago. I'm so glad we still have time to heal this family.

I read your book daily. Thank you. You saved my life by giving me a life more worth living.

Connie
Orlando, FL

My husband and I were concerned with our 5-year-old adopted son. He showed no fear or remorse. He would do things in spite of being told the safe way to do it. He would show no caution. Chad would also say something cruel and not show sadness or concern. He would actually risk it all to show he didn't care and would lose all the things he enjoyed, with no concern for his own wellbeing. I was afraid; I had read some awful reports on this type of behavior.

I wouldn't let anyone babysit. I was scared they would be concerned, too. We love our son so much we were willing to do whatever it takes.

We were just beginning a new parenting approach with Heather Forbes. She positioned us at his level and had us address our own fear. We realized that Chad only acted this way when he was stressed. And in the beginning that was all the time! When we started having less meltdowns or "in the moments," we could see and feel his innocence and love. His compassion and wanting to have fun came bubbling out. He remembers to look both ways and not to say mean things, or when he does he can say "I'm sorry." Our family has been working with the BCI paradigm for three years. It's working.

T.C.
Pinon Hills, CA

Before Beyond Consequences, my 12-year-old son and I had a very tumultuous living arrangement. I say arrangement because I was in the same house as this troubled 12-year-old. This was not a pleasant arrangement at all. We argued about everything and battled about anything. I lost my temper constantly, which caused him to lose his temper constantly. He had poor social skills at home, school, and even at church. It was not a pretty sight! He would get suspended from school at the least provocation, which usually was the result of breaking the school's Code of Conduct laws. These rules addressed infractions, and the consequences for committing infractions stated the number of days of suspension given to any student charged.

Things had grown so horrible through the years, nothing I tried worked. It had gotten so frustrating that an out-of-the-home placement was even considered because I didn't know what else to do. I began using the Beyond Consequences paradigm through an in-home counseling agency, much to my disbelief and frustration. However, after parenting classes, reading the book, attending two Beyond Consequences workshops, meeting the authors of Volume 1, and actually learning to use the paradigm, there was evidence of small growth! Although I didn't see the growth the counselor saw, I continued to try this different method of working with my son. This child, whom I'd rejected at an earlier age due to my own baggage, with whom I used outdated punishment methods, I grew to accept and love. I learned to love him as my son who was in actuality a very scared and angry child deep inside. So many things had been chaotic in both of our lives since his dad had been incarcerated (when he was 5 years old).

His social skills were a mess everywhere he went. He refused to do his homework. He did not want to clean his room. He used profanity when angry. He would steal and did not want to get up and go to school. He became a child with destructive behaviors which caused school suspensions and misunderstandings anywhere and everywhere he went. He was a basket-case and so were his brother and I.

When Beyond Consequences really sank into my every being and when I realized my son was actually afraid and really needed a calm, regulated, loving, parent-relationship with me, his mother, I began to see a different child. I began to see a child, my child, who I could talk to and, yes, accept for who he was. He had not known how to express his fears, and I was too busy with my own fears to know how to help him.

We are continuing to use the Beyond Consequences paradigm and sharing it with key individuals who interact with him. Classroom teachers, principals, church members, neighbors, and parents of children with attachment disorders were given literature and encouraged to practice some of the methods we had learned. Although we still have things to overcome, we have come a very long way. Today, my son and

I are more aware of his behaviors as a result of what we've learned. He has less behavioral issues at school and has improved in his ability to relate to authority figures. I can honestly say that I, too, was afraid and angry and regret the punishment routines I was inflicting on my son, but I didn't know a better method than what my own history contained. We are now living an improved life and have a relationship of love. I know this paradigm works if we work it!

Rhonda
Danville, VA

My 9-year-old adopted son is often exhausted by the end of the day, and bedtimes are not too much of a problem, but sometimes it is all too much for him and he can't handle me coming in to say it is time for bed (especially when his older sister is still up).

One night, his immediate reaction was total rage and very loud aggressive shouting of the "Oh you always do this. You're horrible!" (and probably much worse language) variety. He ran across the room and wedged himself under the stairs so I couldn't reach him. He was red-faced and furious. I went to where he was and tried to speak to him, but he yelled, "Shut up! Shut up! You're so stupid!" and every time I tried to speak, shouted over the top of me to shut up.

At times in the past I would have crawled in and tried to pull him out bodily. I have sometimes had to hold him close until he calms down to stop him from damaging our home or ourselves. But he is getting bigger and stronger every day, and these ugly struggles don't help our relationship at all.

I took a deep breath and thought about how frightened he must be, and how he had quite literally backed himself into a corner from which he couldn't escape. I could see that words were not going to work between us for quite a while. So I smiled at him and gave him a thumbs up sign to indicate that, OK, I wasn't going to speak. Then I used rudimentary sign language, still smiling, to indicate to him that what I would like would be for him to come out, go upstairs, take off his clothes (I mimed all this, with particular emphasis on coyly taking off his underwear), put on his pajamas, brush his teeth, climb into bed and sleep like a baby.

By the time I had finished, he was grinning and beginning to sign back to me. He loved it that we had this private language (his sister was elsewhere in the room). I waved him out from under the stairs with a courtly bow as if a prince was emerging and he trotted upstairs not just cheerfully but with a better connection between us than there had been 10 minutes before.

He ended up being the hero, not the villain, of the story, and I felt happy I had managed a difficult situation so it turned into a good experience for both of us.

Nicola
Norfolk, England

My daughters were 2 years 10 months (Regina) and 18 months old (Alina) when we brought them home from a Russian orphanage. We had no attachment or behavior problems with the Alina. But, our relationship with Regina was difficult from the start. She is very intelligent, spoke Russian very well for her age and was exceptionally scared. I think she still retained if not a clear memory of her birth mother, what I call a memory of a memory...and we were not the people she remembered or missed. We're really nice people, gentle and calm, we speak some Russian, I had read lots about attachment issues, but still it was not the right information.

Over the years we got to what I call a negotiated settlement. We'd go weeks doing just fine, and then, probably because we'd expand our horizons thinking all was well, she'd revert to all the difficult behaviors. All along, even when we were not having conflict, I longed for the deep connectedness we both have with our younger. I couldn't wait to wake up Alina in the morning, I dreaded that first encounter with Regina. I was thrilled to watch Alina come out of class and look for me, see me and come running. I dreaded collecting Regina. And I felt horrible about feeling this way. In retrospect, I see the negative feedback loops we were living.

Her behavior at school was exemplary, she was known as a peacemaker between the kids. She's honest and sincere...but oh could she be defiant with me. Even in first grade I'd struggle with her and homework and defiance...none of which her teacher ever saw, until the end of that school year. With about three weeks to go, her teacher greeted me after school with a conspiratorial air, saying, "I finally saw what you've been talking about... pure defiance." It blew the teacher away since Regina had NEVER shown this at school. We talked about things: it was the end of school and the sadness that this teacher would not be her teacher next year was driving Regina to reject this person who had meant so much to her...self-protection and the defense of defiance.

We bounced along for almost six years. Heather Forbes was giving a short talk nearby (Arcadia, CA) and I went to the talk. It was amazing. It was as if she knew my daughter without ever having met her. After the formal talk, Heather spent about five minutes chatting with me and explained I should read the chapter on defiance and give it a try. Her warmth and sincerity, her confidence in her theory, and her insights into my daughter gave me the courage to take yet another "leap of faith in adoption," that phrase so many of us hear when we are in the process.

I got the book, I read Chapter Five and....well I count our lives together as the time before that night and the time since. Understanding that all her irritating behavior was about her early trauma, not efforts to push me away because she was afraid to love (or any of the other negative messages parents get about kids with these struggles) totally freed me to change what we were doing. I always say the person who changed the most was and is me. I am back to being the person I was when I was much younger, when I assumed I'd be a mom and I'd be fun and do cool things with our kids. The stress of infertility and the fear-filled process of adoption drained me. I became the person who looked at the world through lenses of love rather than fear. Once I understood both Regina's driving forces and my own, our lives changed so smoothly that it is difficult for me to remember specifics.

Some practical skills I used: If I was feeling stressed by incessant chatter from the back seat, I'd say, "Kids, I'm really feeling stressed, we have a lot to get done and I should have done some of this while you were in school. I'm sorry I didn't budget my time better, but I really need your help to get these chores done on the way home," and it was like magic. They would stop fussing, Regina would focus, ask me what I did during the day, say something sweet about what I did get done (like going on field trips with her class) and we'd breeze thru the afternoon. I learned

that her spacey tuning out was self-preservation, not ignoring or reject-
ing me. This allowed me to reach her in other ways. The best tool I have
for staying in regulation with my wonderful, now 11-year-old, is to go
in and lay down with her in the morning, snuggle her awake. I remember the first week I dedicated myself to doing this, whether I felt like
it or not! By Wednesday of that week I ran into a resource teacher at
school, someone who interacted with Regina often but not her classroom
teacher, and she commented, "Wow, Regina is a different kid this week,
I don't know what's different but she's paying attention, she's participating, her speech is clear and on target!" And I had the soft, loving,
accepting child I'd always wanted. She is a remarkable person. I not only
love her, but respect her and am sometimes in awe of her compassion,
her depth of soul, her embodiment of love. Regina is part of my support
now, not my target, and I love her more than I imagined I ever could just
a few years ago.

MaryAlice
Pasadena, CA

As a single woman, I adopted my daughter when she was 3½ years old.
She recently turned 11. Since the time she came home, it has been very
hard for her to get ready for bed. She would sing, dance, act out scenes
from her day, or tell stories. She would try to buy time constantly by
trying to engage me with the typical "one more time" – whether it be
a game, a song, etc. In particular, she would focus on not brushing her
teeth, saying, "I'll brush really well in the morning." This was the last
thing she would do before going to bed (or before leaving the house).
As the time ticked away, it was getting later and later into the night,
my negotiations with her, taking away of privileges, and general argu-
ments between us would start. This behavior had waxed and waned
over the years, but was always interfering and very anxiety producing
for both of us. I had heard about Beyond Consequences and finally
purchased it. I skimmed it one evening, intending to start reading it
one night when I "had time." Bedtime that night started heading right
down the tubes.

Then I thought about what I had just read in Beyond Consequences.
She was scared, but of what? I sat down with her that night and started
talking. She told me she did not want to brush her teeth because after

she brushed I left her. I minimally acknowledged that and said I was "just" downstairs. She agreed that I wasn't really leaving her but that "you really are leaving me." Wow! She was right...I was leaving her! I quickly acknowledged her fear and asked how I could help. She said she wanted me in the bathroom with her. I agreed and sat on the side of the tub (I was tired, too!). Then she turned and asked me to hold her hand while she brushed! I did and she was calm, brushed her teeth, and went to bed. The same scenario was repeated in the morning before leaving for school. Wonderful! This was about two months ago and after about three or four days of hand holding she now would occasionally ask me to either be in the bathroom with her or to hold her hand. Bedtimes are not perfect, believe me, but they feel "typical" to me now!

A few days after the breakthrough evening, I asked my daughter to brush her teeth so we could walk the dog. As soon as I asked her to do this, the anxiety started for me. But then I remembered our new way of handling teeth brushing and leaving. As I smartly trotted behind her to the bathroom, fully intending to be present, she stopped and asked me what I was doing. I quickly reminded her that I could hold her hand and be with her if she needed me. She replied that I did not need to be with her: "Momma, we are leaving together!" Silly me!

Robin
Charlottesville, VA

My 9-year-old son and I had spent the entire morning together, just the two of us. We had gone to Starbucks, therapy, and then we went to the store. My son did a fabulous job of staying calm, with my help, while he selected something to spend his allowance on. We then met my husband for lunch at a restaurant. Things were going fabulously! I decided to take my son swimming and give my husband a little time to take a nap. So we came home and changed clothes, then headed to the pool. At the last minute, I decided to run to the store and get a toy boat that he'd been asking for (it was a whole $1.50). He was so happy about that. We went to the pool, all was well, and then I decided to hit Sonic for an ice cream on the way home. What a nice day it had been!

We arrived home and he ate his ice cream. He played a game with my husband and then headed out to play with a friend. His friend wasn't home, so he came back and when I saw the look on his face, I knew where we were headed. I turned around and pulled him to me and asked him what was wrong. He quickly decided he wanted to do a craft with me. I was right in the middle of cleaning the kitchen, so I told him when I was done, we would do something. That wasn't good enough. He turned and started to head out of the room. I tried to get a hold of him and hug him (that usually works to calm him) but he wanted none of it. He stormed off into his room. I calmly followed (forcing myself to take deep breaths and not start yelling at him, or FORCE him to hug me to calm him down). He saw me follow him and he turned to face me as he shut his door in my face. I can quite honestly say that in the past, I'd have NEVER allowed that door to be shut in my face, but this time something clicked for me. I stood outside his door and took a deep breath. I could hear him just on the other side of it. I'm quite sure he was braced against it just waiting for me to start forcing the door open. I quietly and calmly said "I'm not going to push your door open. When you are ready for me to come in, I'll be waiting right here." He immediately said "you can come in" and he turned the doorknob for me.

I went in and he started throwing things, kicking things, his beanbag chair included, then he flopped down on it and started to scream and cry. He screamed "You NEVER have time to do things with me! You are always working!" In the old way, I would have begun listing all the things we had done together, starting off with Starbucks together at 7:00 that morning, but, instead, I somehow remained quite calm and I lay down beside him on that bean bag chair and said "Oh, Shane, I am so sorry." He continued with "You always have work to do, and you never have time to do anything with me!" I simply stated again how sorry I was and that he looked so sad and possibly angry at me. He continued his rant and I continued to apologize and reflect what I saw in his eyes. He turned and looked me in the eyes. I believe he saw that I was truly sincere. He slowly reached up and caressed my face and said, "It's alright, Mommy." I just remained silent and lightly rubbed his arm, and from time to time, his face. I then said, "I think we need to do something together. The kitchen can wait." (This was after a good 10 minutes of me just laying there and showing him I had nowhere to go.) He said, "No, it's okay. I know you need to do that." I said, "No, you are more important than that, so what would you like to do?"

So, we spent a few minutes together, and he ended up wanting to go outside and play without me, but, wow...what a difference! He is now regulated, as am I, and I am feeling pretty good about that whole inter- action. I've seen it firsthand; this works! I was able to take my son from a state of extreme dysregulation to a calm and regulated state all by simply staying connected and validating his feelings. The life lessons will come, I trust in that, and I'm not worried because THIS is truly parenting out of love.

Twyla
Leander, Texas

Although my 15-year-old son was initially excited about an upcom- ing trip to the beach in Mexico, he quickly became angry and anxious, demanding to be allowed to stay home alone. That obviously wasn't an option but as the time to go approached his emotions were swinging wildly. I was afraid he might physically refuse to go and was starting to get pretty angry and anxious myself especially since the trip was planned with him in mind as something I thought he would love. I realized his limited experience with vacations in the past with his fam- ily of origin had involved his biological sister getting high on meth and beating him to a bloody pulp. The day before we left, we had a long talk about what he might need to make him feel safer and more comfort- able on the trip. We went shopping and I bought him the things he thought he would need as well as a swimsuit which he insisted he wouldn't need as he was planning to spend the whole trip in our room. I decided just getting him there was going to be enough of a success; we would deal with things as they came up and anything good that happened would just be gravy.

We arrived at this incredibly beautiful condo we had rented and he just exploded. He was furious and sobbing. I quickly sent my other children down to the beach and tried to go to him. He told me to "get the hell away" from him and was banging on doors and swearing about "this shithole." My gut reaction was to get angry but I recognized it for what it was and started talking to him about fear. I talked about how scary it was to be in a completely unfamiliar place with none of the things he was used to around. I talked about how scary it was to feel so out of control about what was happening. I told him he was safe and that I was always going to keep him safe. I said that when he felt a little bit safer he might want to go do some things but I would stay in the condo with him until he was ready and that if he was never ready that was okay too. In an amazingly short time he was down on the beach in the swimsuit he swore he wouldn't need. There were plenty of ups and downs that week but I just kept focusing on the fear and in the end our entire family had a wonderful vacation.

Deborah
Albuquerque, NM

Two weeks ago, I called our county mental health agency and said that after 10 years with my 11-year-old daughter, adopted from Romania at 15 months old, I could not go on. The therapist told me about Beyond Consequences, so I got the book, read it, and read through the material on your website. Immediately, I UNDERSTOOD and I DID IT!

Two weeks later, a miracle has happened. I am now, finally, calm and under control. And, my daughter has attached to me. This is the first time in 10 years of therapists, doctors, psychiatrists, psychologists – none of whom could help!

Love,
Mary
Lynchburg, VA

Endnotes

A Note to the Reader

[1] Shilts, D. (1999). *Love is a start*. Portland, OR: Look Again Publishing.

[2] Thomas, N.L. (1997). *When love is not enough: a guide to parenting children with RAD-reactive attachment disorder*. Glenwood Springs, CO: Nancy Thomas.

[3] Loux, A.K. (1997). *The limits of hope: An adoptive mother's story*. Charlottesville, VA: University Press of Virginia.

Chapter 3 – Staying Present in the Moment

[1] Siegel, D. (2007). Keynote address, Neuroscience Meets Recovery, 2nd Annual Conference. Las Vegas, NV.

[2] Covey, S.R. (2007). *The 8th Habit: From Effectiveness to Greatness*. New York, NY: Free Press.

[3] Goldman. D. (2006). *Social Intelligence*. New York, NY: Bantam Books.

[4] Goleman, D. (n.d.). Retrieved August 4, 2008, from http://www.danielgoleman.info.

[5] Siegel, D. (2007). Keynote address, Neuroscience Meets Recovery, 2nd Annual Conference. Las Vegas, NV.

[6] *Wikipedia*. Wikimedia Foundation, Inc. Retrieved August 3, 2008 from http://en.wikipedia.org/wiki/Intuition_%28knowledge%29.

[7] Siegel, D. (2007). Keynote address, Neuroscience Meets Recovery, 2nd Annual Conference. Las Vegas, NV.

[8] Tolle, E. (2004). *The Power of Now: A Guide to Spiritual Enlightenment*. Novato, CA: New World Library.

Chapter 4 – Our Parenting Programs

[1] Assaraf, J.J. (n.d.) *Recondition your mind*. (MP3 download). One Coach (www.onecoach.com).

[2] Ibid.

[3] Solomon, M.F. & Siegel, D.J. (Eds.). (2003). *Healing trauma: Attachment, mind, body, and brain*. New York, NY: W.W. Norton & Company..

[4] Lipton, B.H. (2005). *The biology of belief: Unleashing the power of the consciousness matter and miracles*. Santa Rosa, CA: Mountain of Love/Elite Books.

[5] Ibid.

[6] Forbes, H.T. & Dziegielewski, S. (2003). Issues facing adoptive mothers of children with special needs. *Journal of Social Work 3*(3).

[7] Martin, A. & Landrell J. (2005). *Energy psychology / energy medicine: The practice of neuro-kinesiology and psychoneuroimmunology in exploring the mind/body connection*. Penryn, CA: Personal Transformation Press.

[8] Perry, B.D. & Pollard, R. (1998). Homeostasis, stress, trauma and adaptation: A neurodevelopmental view of childhood trauma. *Child and Adolescent Psychiatric Clinics of North America, 7*(1) 33-51.

Chapter 5 – Window of Stress Tolerance

[1] Selye, H. (1974). *Stress without distress*. New York, NY: Signet.

[2] Ibid.

[3] Solomon, M.F. & Siegel, D.J. (Eds.). (2003). *Healing trauma: Attachment, mind, body, and brain*. New York, NY: W.W. Norton & Company.

[4] Assaraf, J. (2007). *Having it all: Achieving your life's goals and dreams*. Simon & Schuster.

[5] Solomon, M.F. & Siegel, D.J. (Eds.). (2003). *Healing trauma: Attachment, mind, body, and brain*. New York, NY: W.W. Norton & Company.

Chapter 6 – Expectations

[1] Santa Barbara Graduate Institute (2004). *Trauma, brain, and relationship: Helping children heal* [DVD].

Chapter 7 – Poor Social Skills

[1] Lipton, B.H. (2005). *The biology of belief: Unleashing the power of the consciousness matter and miracles*. Santa Rosa, CA: Mountain of Love/Elite Books.

[2] Ibid.

[3] MindDisorders.com (n.d.) *Social skills training*. Retrieved June 20, 2008, from http://www.minddisorders.com/Py-Z/Social-skills-training.html.

[4] National Association of School Psychologists (n.d.) Social skills: Promoting positive behavior, academic success, and school safety. Retrieved June 20, 2008, from http://www.nasponline.org/resources/factsheets/socialskills_fs.aspx.

[5] Lipton, B.H. (2005). *The biology of belief: Unleashing the power of the consciousness matter and miracles*. Santa Rosa, CA: Mountain of Love/Elite Books.

[6] Corbin, J.R. (2007). Reactive attachment disorder: A biopsychosocial disturbance of attachment. *Child Adolescent Social Work Journal,* 24:539-552.

[7] Goleman, D. (2006). *Social intelligence: The new science of human relationships*. New York, NY: Bantam Dell.

[8] Egan, S.K. & Perry, D.G. (1998). Does low self-regard invite victimization? *Developmental Psychology,* Vol. 34 (2): 299-309.

[9] Bowlby, J. (1973). *Separation: Anxiety and anger (Attachment and Loss Vol 2)*. New York, NY: Basic Books.

[10] Ojanen, T. & Perry, D.G. (2007). Relational schemas and the developing self: Perceptions of mother and of self as joint predictors of early adolescents' self-esteem. *Developmental Psychology,* Vol. 43 (6): 1474-1483.

[11] Ibid.

[12] Goleman, D. (2006). *Social intelligence: The new science of human relationships*. New York, NY: Bantam Dell.

Chapter 8 – Demanding

[1] University of Michigan Health System (2006). Spoiled children: Prevention. Retrieved February 12, 2008, from http://www.med.umich.edu/1libr/pa/pa_prevspo_hhg.htm.

[2] Ibid.

[3] AllAboutParenting.com (n.d.). *Discipline for strong-willed child*. Retrieved February 12, 2008, from http://www.allaboutparenting.org/discipline-for-strong-willed-child-faq.htm.

[4] University of Michigan Health System (2006). *Spoiled children: Prevention*. Retrieved February 12, 2008, from http://www.med.umich.edu/1libr/pa/pa_prevspo_hhg.htm.

[5] Dobson, J. (1992). *The new dare to discipline*. Carol Stream, IL: Tyndale House Publisher.

[6] Ibid.

[7] Ibid.

[8] Ooi, Y.P.; Ang, R.P.; Fund, D.S.; Wong, G.; & Cai, Y. (2006). *The impact of parent-child attachment on aggression, social stress, and self-esteem*. School Psychology International, Vol. 27(5); 552-566.

[8] Ibid., p. 553.

Chapter 9 – Self Injury

[1] Perry, B. & Szalavitz, M. (2007). *The boy who was raised as a dog: And other stories from a child psychiatrist's notebook – What traumatized children can teach us about loss, love, and healing*. New York, NY: Basic Books.

[2] Van der Kolk, Perry, and Herman (1991). Childhood origins of self-destructive behavior. *The American Journal of Psychiatry,* Vol. 148 (12), 1665-1674.

[3] Smith, B.D. (2008). Adolescent nonsuicidal self-injury: Evaluation and treatment. Why do adolescents self-injure and what are the therapeutic options for treating them? *Psychiatric Times,* 25 (7).

[4] Ibid.

[5] Ibid.

[6] Sachsse, U., Von Der Heyde, S., & Huether, G. (2007). Stress regulation and self-mutilation. *American Journal of Psychiatry,* 159 (4), 672.

[7] Perry, B. & Szalavitz M. (2006). *The boy who was raised as a dog: And other stories from a child psychiatrist's notebook – What traumatized children can teach us about loss, love, and healing.* New York, NY: Basic Books.

Chapter 10 – Defensive Attitudes

[1] Medicinenet.com (2004). *Changing Your Child's Attitude.* Retreived March 28, 2008, from http://www.medicinenet.com/script/main/art.asp?articlekey=53671.

[2] Leman, K. (2008). *Have a new kid by Friday; How to change your child's attitude, behavior, and character in five days.* Grand Rapids, MI: Revell.

[3] Ibid.

Chapter 11 – No Conscience

[1] Magid, K., & McKelvey C.A. (1987). *High-risk children without a conscience.* New York, NY: Bantam Books.

[2] Thomas, N.L. (1997). *When love is not enough: A guide to parenting children with RAD-reactive attachment disorder.* Glenwood Springs, CO: Nancy Thomas.

[3] Cline, F.W., & Helding, C. (1999). *Can this child be saved?* Franksville, WI: World Enterprises.

[4] Delaney, R.J. (1998). *Fostering changes: Treating attachment-disordered foster children.* Oklahoma City, OK: Wood 'N' Barnes Publishing.

[5] Randolph, E. (1997). *Children who shock and surprise: A guide to attachment disorders.* Evergreen, CO: PDQ Printing.

[6] Hughes, D.A. (1997). *Facilitating developmental attachment: The road to emotional recovery and behavioral change in foster and adopted children.* Northvale, NJ: Jason Aronson, Inc.

[7] Orlans, M., & Levy, T.M. (2006). *Healing parents: Helping wounded children learn to trust and love.* Washington, D.C.: CWLA Press.

[8] Buenning, W.D. (n.d.). *Attachment symptoms.* Retrieved September 23, 2007, from http://www.reactiveattachmentdisordertreatment.com/ssi/article2.html.

[9] Orlans, M., & Levy, T.M. (2006). *Healing parents: Helping wounded children learn to trust and love.* Washington, D.C.: CWLA Press.

[10] Levy, T.M., & Orlans, M. (1998). *Attachment, trauma, and healing: Understanding and treating attachment disorder in children and families.* Washington, D.C.: CWLA Press.

[11] Hare, R.D. (1999). *Without conscience: The disturbing world of the psychopaths among us*. New York, NY: The Guilford Press.

[12] Hare, R.D. (1993). *Without conscience: The disturbing world of psychopaths among us*. New York, NY: The Guilford Press.

[13] Magid, K., & McKelvey C.A. (1987). *High-risk children without a conscience*. New York, NY: Bantam Books.

[14] Ibid.

[15] Cassel, E. & Bernstein, D.A. (2001). *Criminal behavior*. Boston, MA: Allyn and Bacon.

[16] Perry, B. & Szalavitz, M. (2006). *The boy who was raised as a dog: And other stories from a child psychiatrist's notebook*. New York, NY: Basic Books.

[17] Lipton, B.H. (2005). *The biology of belief: Unleashing the power of the consciousness matter and miracles*. Santa Rosa, CA: Mountain of Love/Elite Books.

[18] Ibid.

[19] Burns, J. (n.d.). *Garbage in / garbage out: The influences of media on your self-esteem*. Retrieved September 25, 2007, from http://homeword.com/Articles/ArticleDetail.aspx?iArticleId=74.

[20] Lipton, B.H. (2005). *The biology of belief: Unleashing the power of the consciousness matter and miracles*. Santa Rosa, CA: Mountain of Love/Elite Books.

[21] *Wikipedia*. Wikimedia Foundation, Inc. Retrieved October 25, 2007, from http://en.wikipedia.org/wiki/Selfishness.

[22] Hare, R.D. (1993). *Without conscience: The disturbing world of psychopaths among us*. New York, NY: The Guilford Press.

Chapter 12 – Homework

[1] The Franklin Institute (n.d.). *Stress and Memory*. Retrieved August 4, 2008, from http://www.fi.edu/learn/brain/stress.html#stressmemory.

[2] Meltz, B.F. (2002). *How Parents Can Help Remove Homework Hurdles*. Retrieved June 3, 2008, from http://www.middleweb.com/INCASEhomewktips.html.

[3] Thomas, N.L. (1997). *Teacher resources: Homework*. Retrieved June 4, 2008, from http://www.attachment.org/pages_teachers_homework.php.

[4] Bright Futures (n.d.). *Homework problems*. Retrieved June 2, 2008, from http://www.brightfutures.org/mentalhealth/pdf/professionals/mc/homework.pdf.

[5] MacKenzie, R.J. (2001). *Setting limits with your strong-willed child: Eliminating conflict by establishing clear, firm, and respectful boundaries*. New York, NY: Three Rivers Press.

[6] Meltz, B.F. (2002). *How Parents Can Help Remove Homework Hurdles.* Retrieved June 3, 2008, from http://www.middleweb.com/INCASEhomewktips. html.

[7] Ibid.

[8] Arnsten, A.F. (1998). Development of the cerebral cortex: XIV. Stress impairs prefrontal cortical function. *American Academy of Child Adolescent Psychiatry, 37*(12): 1337-1339.

[9] *Homework for primary pupils should be scrapped.* (2008). Retrieved June 8, 2008, from http://www.timesonline.co.uk/tol/news/uk/education/article3525626.ece).

[10] Kohn, A. (2007). Rethinking homework. *Principal.*

[11] Bowlby, J. (1988). *A secure base: Parent-child attachment and healthy development.* New York, NY: Basic Books.

[12] MacKenzie, R.J. (2001). *Setting limits with your strong-willed child: Eliminating conflict by establishing clear, firm, and respectful boundaries.* New York, NY: Three Rivers Press.

Chapter 13 – Chores

[1] Rose, V.L. (1998). AAP issues policy statement on parental discipline of children. *American Family Physician.*

[2] Leman, K. (2008). *Have a new kid by Friday: How to change your child's attitude, behavior, and character in five days.* Grand Rapids, MI: Revell.

[3] Ibid.

[4] Adopting.org (n.d.). *Techniques that work.* Retrieved July 15, 2008, from http://www.adopting.org/adoptions/reactive-attachment-disorder-techniques-that-work.html.

5 Thomas, N.L. (1997). *When love is not enough: A guide to parenting children with RAD-reactive attachment disorder.* Glenwood Springs, CO: Nancy Thomas.

[6] Hage, D. (n.d.). *Guiding philosophy of attachment therapy.* Retrieved July 15, 2008, from http://www.childrenintherapy.org/proponents/hage.html.

[7] Williams, D. (n.d.). *Attachment disorder.* Retrieved July 9, 2008, from http://www.helponechild.org/resources/pcc/dr_williams_attachment.html.

[8] Bowlby, R. (Producer). (n.d.). *Attachment: Three educational videos* [VHS tape] London, UK.

Recommended Readings
■

Resources for Parents:

Brazelton, T.B. (1992). *Touchpoints: Your child's emotional and behavioral development*. Reading, MA: Addison-Wesley Publishing.

Brazelton, T.B. & Greenspan, S. (2000). *The irreducible needs of children: What every child must have to grow, learn, and flourish*. Cambridge, MA: Perseus Publishing.

Breggin, P. (2000). *Reclaiming our children: A healing solution for a nation in crisis*. Cambridge, MA: Perseus Books.

Chopra, D. (1994). *Journey into healing*. New York: Harmony Books.

Clark, N. & Post, B. (2005). *The forever child: A tale of loss and impossible dreams*. Mountain View, OK: M. Brynn Publishing.

Clark, N. & Post, B. (2003). *The forever child: A tale of fear and anger*. Mountain View, OK: M. Brynn Publishing.

Clark, N. & Post, B. (2002). *The forever child: A tale of lies and love*. Mountain View, OK: M. Brynn Publishing.

Covey, S.R. (2007). *The 8th habit: From effectiveness to greatness*. New York, NY: Free Press.

Davis, P. (1999). *The power of touch: The basis for survival, health, intimacy, and emotional well-being*. Carlsbad, CA: Hay House.

Eldridge, S. (1999). *Twenty things adopted kids wish their adoptive parents knew*. New York, NY: Dell Publishing.

Forbes, H.T. & Post, B.B. (2006). *Beyond consequences, logic, and control: A love-based approach to helping attachment-challenged children with severe behaviors,* Volume I. Orlando, FL: BCI.

Forbes, H.T. & Dziegielewski, S. (2003). *Issues facing adoptive mothers of children with special needs*. Journal of Social Work 3 (3). (Available for download at: www.beyondconsequences.com)

Goldman. D. (2006). *Social Intelligence*. New York, NY: Bantam Books.

Goleman, D. (1994). *Emotional intelligence: Why it can matter more than IQ*. New York, NY: Bantam Books.

Granju, K. & Kennedy, B. (1999). *Attachment parenting: Instinctive care for your baby and young child*. New York, NY: Pocket Books.

Hanh, T. (1987). *Being peace*. Berkeley, CA: Parallax Press.

Harris, B. (2008). *Confident parents, remarkable kids: 8 principles for raising kids you'll love to live with*. Avon, MA: Adams Media.

Harris, B. (2003). *When your kids push your buttons and what you can do about it*. New York, NY: Warner Books.

Hanessian, L. (2004). *Let the baby drive: Navigating the road of new motherhood*. New York, NY: St. Martin's Press.

Hart, A. (1992). *Stress and your child*. Dallas, TX: Word Publishing.

Jamplosky, G. (1979). *Love is letting go of fear*. Berkley, CA: Celestial Arts.

Karen, R. (1994). *Becoming attached: Unfolding the mystery of the infant-mother bond and its impact on later life*. New York, NY: Warner Books, Inc.

Karr-Morse, R., & Wiley, M.S. (1997). *Ghosts from the nursery: Tracing the roots of violence*. New York: Atlantic Monthly Press.

Kohn, A. (2006). *The homework myth: Why our kids get too much of a bad thing*. Cambridge, MA: Da Capo Press.

Kohn, A. (2005). *Unconditional parenting: Moving from rewards and punishment to love and reason*. New York, NY: Atria Books.

Liedloff, J. (1986). *The continuum concept*. New York, NY: Penguin Books.

Perry, B. & Szalavitz M. (2007). *The boy who was raised as a dog: And other stories from a child psychiatrist's notebook – What traumatized children can teach us about loss, love, and healing*. New York, NY: Basic Books.

Rosenberg, M. (2003). *Nonviolent communication: A language of life*. Encinitas, CA: Puddle Dancer Press.

Sears, W. & Sears, M. (2001). *The attachment parenting book: A commonsense guide to understanding and nurturing your baby*. New York, NY: Little, Brown and Company.

Selye, H. (1974). *Stress without distress*. New York, NY: Signet.

Siegel, D. & Hartzell, M. (2003). *Parenting from the inside-out: How a deeper self-understanding can help you raise children who thrive.* New York, NY: Jeremy P. Tarcher/ Putnam.

Tolle, E. (1999). *The power of now.* Novato, CA: New World Library.

Verrier, N.N. (1993). *The primal wound: Understanding the adopted child.* Baltimore, MD: Gateway Press.

Additional Resources for Professionals:

Bowlby, J. (1988). *A secure base: Parent-child attachment and healthy human development.* New York, NY: Basic Books.

Bowlby, J. (1980). *Attachment and loss: Vol. 3 Loss: Sadness and depression.* New York: Basic Books.

Bowlby, J. (1973). *Attachment and loss: Vol. 2 Separation and anger.* New York, NY: Basic Books.

Bowlby, J. (1969). *Attachment and loss: Vol.1 Attachment.* New York, NY: Basic Books.

Bremner, J. (2002). *Does stress damage the brain?: Understanding trauma-related disorders from a mind-body perspective.* New York, NY: W.W. Norton and Company.

Carnegie Corporation (1994). *Starting point: Meeting the needs of our youngest children: The report of the Carnegie task force on meeting the needs of young children.* New York, NY: Carnegie Corporation of New York.

DeGangi, Georgia. (2000). *Pediatric disorders of regulation in affect and behavior.* New York, NY: Academic Press.

Frattaroli, E. (2001). *Healing the soul in the age of the brain.* New York, NY: Penguin Books.

Greenspan, S., and Cunningham, A. (1993, August 22). *Where do violent kids come from?* Charlotte Observer, reprinted in the Washington Post.

Janus, L. (1997). *Echoes from the womb.* Livingston, NY: Jason Aronson.

Justice, B., & Justice, R. (1990). *The abusing family.* New York, NY: Plenum Press.

Kandel, E.R. (1998). *A new intellectual framework for psychiatry*. American Journal of Psychiatry, 155, 457-469.

LeDoux, J. (1996). *The emotional brain: The mysterious underpinnings of emotional life*. New York, NY: Touchstone.

Levine, P.A. (1999). *Healing trauma: Restoring the wisdom of the body*. (Audio Cassette Recording). Louisville, CO: Sounds True, Inc.

Levine, P.A. (1997). *Waking the tiger, healing trauma*. Berkley, CA: North Atlantic Books.

Lipton, B. (2005). *The biology of belief: Unleashing the power of consciousness, matter, and miracles*. Santa Rosa, CA: Mountain of Love/Elite Books.

McEwen, B.S. (1992). Paradoxical effects of adrenal steroids on the brain: Protection vs. degeneration. *Biological Psychiatry 31*, 177-199.

McEwen, B. (1999). Development of the cerebral cortex XIII: Stress and brain development – II. *Journal of the American Academy of Child and Adolescent Psychiatry, 38*, 101-103.

Montagu, A. (1986). *Touching: The human significance of the skin*. New York, NY: Harper and Row.

National Center for Clinical Infant Programs (2005). *Diagnostic classification of mental health and developmental disorders of infancy and early childhood*. Arlington, VA: Zero to Three.

Perry, B.D. (2002). Childhood experience and the expression of genetic potential: What childhood neglect tells us about nature and nurture. *Brain and Mind, 3*, 79-100.

Perry, B.D. & Pollard, R. (1998). Homeostasis, stress, trauma and adaptation: A neurodevelopmental view of childhood trauma. *Child and Adolescent Psychiatric Clinics of North America, 7*(1) 33-51.

Perry, B.D. (1997). Incubated in terror: Neurodevelopmental factors in the "cycle of violence." In J. Osofsky (Ed.), *Children in a violent society* (pp. 124-149). New York, NY: Guilford Press.

Perry, B.D. (1996). *Maltreated children: Experience, brain development, and the next generation*. New York, NY: W. W. Norton.

Perry, B.D. (1996). *Neurodevelopmental adaptations to violence: How children survive the intergenerational vortex of violence, Violence and childhood trauma: Understanding and responding to the effects of violence on young children,* Gund Foundation, Cleveland.

Perry, B.D., Pollard, R.A., Blakely, T.L. Baker, W.L., & Vigilante, D. (1995). Childhood trauma, the neurobiology of adaptation, and "use-dependent" development of the brain: How states become traits. *Infant Mental Health Journal, 16,* 271-291.

Perry, B.D. (1993). Neurodevelopment and the neurophysiology of trauma: Conceptual considerations for clinical work with maltreated children. *The Advisor, American Professional Society on the Abuse of Children,* 6:1.

Pert, C.B. (2004). *Your body is your subconscious mind* (Audio CD Recording). Louisville, CO: Soundstrue, Inc.

Pert, C.B. (2004). *Psychosomatic wellness: Healing your bodymind* (Audio CD Recording). Magic Bullets, Inc.

Pert, C.B. (1997). *Molecules of emotion.* New York, NY: Touchstone.

Ross, C.A. (2000). *The trauma model.* Richardson, TX: Manitou Communications.

Sapolsky, R.M. (1990). Stress in the wild. *Scientific American 262,* 116-23.

Scaer, R.C. (2005). *The trauma spectrum: Hidden wounds and human resiliency.* New York, NY: W.W. Norton & Company, Inc.

Schore, A.N. (1994). *Affect regulation and the origin of the self.* Hillsdale, NJ: Lawrence Erlbaum Associates, Publishers.

Schore, A.N. (2003). *Affect regulation and the repair of the self.* New York, NY: W.W. Norton.

Shapiro, F. & Forrest, M. (1998). *EMDR: The breakthrough therapy for overcoming anxiety, stress, and trauma.* New York, NY: Basic Books.

Siegel, D.J. (1995a). Memory, trauma, and psychotherapy: A cognitive science view. *Journal of Psychotherapy Practice and Research, 4,* 93-122.

Solomon, M.F. & Siegel, D.J. (Eds.). (2003). *Healing trauma: Attachment, mind, body, and brain.* New York, NY: W.W. Norton & Company.

Index

■

love 3, 5, 7, 10, 16, 21, 34, 61, 71, 83, 90, 94, 130

manipulation 28, 110, 129
mealtime 132
memory 12. 17, 19, 25-26, 116, 118, 154

neglect 49, 51, 60, 70, 77, 80, 121
neocortex 9, 12, 16, 18-19, 68, 104, 113, 118,
neurological 17, 19, 24, 26, 36, 40, 69, 93, 104, 122, 127, 134
neuroscience 12, 16, 36, 61, 105

oppositional defiant disorder 103, 117

pain 2, 6, 16, 17, 51, 66-67, 71, 76, 79, 81-85, 87, 90, 100, 102, 109, 139
paradigm 28, 36, 49, 54, 93-94, 106, 152
parenting 2-7, 9-10, 12-13, 17, 19, 23, 26, 37, 52, 54, 66-67, 71, 78-79, 90, 92, 94, 106,
    109, 117, 131-132, 134-136, 141, 159
personal power 19, 29
playtime 57, 124, 132
power of love 85
power struggles 65, 132
prefrontal cortex 12, 118
punishment 66, 76, 84, 88, 113, 132, 152-153

rage 35, 153
react 3, 12, 15, 24-26, 30, 43, 65, 68, 78, 85, 107-108
reaction 15, 70, 27, 29, 31, 49, 51, 68, 70-71, 83-84, 85-86, 88-89, 93, 104, 135, 142,
    146, 153, 159
reactive attachment disorder (RAD) 1, 3 101, 117
reptilian brain 7-9, 25, 104-105, 113,
regulation 12-14, 18, 35-36, 38, 51, 53, 56-57, 70-71, 76, 108, 120-121, 128, 141, 156
regulatory system 14, 92, 126
responsibility 7, 9, 13, 23-24, 28-30, 40, 50, 53, 70, 72, 74, 83, 93, 96-98, 103, 111,
    115-117, 127-128, 132-134, 144, 146
resistance 80, 90, 122, 124, 126, 139, 142, 146

safety 4, 7, 14, 16, 19, 51-52, 56, 60-61, 70-72, 76, 90, 93-96, 103-104, 106, 109, 111,
    122, 136-138
school 24, 37, 42, 48, 54, 57, 60, 65, 67, 73-75, 98, 115-119, 122, 124-125, 129, 134,
    151-157
self-regulation 6, 38, 92
short-term memory 116
siblings 22, 57, 102, 107, 109, 113
stress response system 7, 18
survival 7-9, 15-17, 23-25, 60, 69, 89-90, 103-106, 109, 111, 113, 116, 121-122, 134,
    136, 138-139

threat 18, 57, 62, 79, 89, 91, 93, 100, 103-104, 106-109, 111, 113, 116, 121, 126-127, 130
trust 3-4, 11, 19, 53, 83, 85, 88, 92. 94, 123, 126, 159

window of tolerance 13, 33-38, 43, 56, 65, 68, 116, 120, 137

Check out the
Beyond Consequences Institute
website today to:
■

- Sign-up on our network and receive announcements of future free events such as teleseminars and lectures.

- Receive Heather's free eNewsletter for more Q&A support.

- Download free articles that will further your understanding of the Beyond Consequences Model.

- Learn how you can have Heather T. Forbes, LCSW in your area to hold a seminar or workshop.

- Purchase additional copies of this book for teachers, friends, and family members.

- View videos of how this model works when parents make the commitment to move from fear to love.

www.beyondconsequences.com

Order Form
∎

Books	Quantity	Cost	Total
Beyond Consequences, Logic, and Control: ***A Love-Based Approach to Helping*** ***Attachment-Challenged Children with*** ***Severe Behaviors***	———	———	———

    1 to 4 copies: $19.95 each
    5 to 10 copies: $17.95 each
    11 to 25 copies: $15.95 each
    26 to 50 copies: $13.95 each
    (Prices good for both Volumes 1 and 2)

Dare to Love	———	———	———

    (Prices same as above)

100 Daily Parenting Reflections ***A Love-Based Parenting Nuggets to*** ***Encourage You Daily***	———	———	———

    $9.95 each

DVD

Beyond Consequences Live!	———	———	———

4-set DVD
If you've been unable to attend a Beyond Consequences Live training event, here is your solution. Intensive role plays on this dynamic DVD will give you "real-life" examples to equip you as a parent with "real-life" solutions.
    $109.00 each

Audio CD's

Beyond Consequences for ***Toddlers, 5 to 9's, Tweens, Teenagers***	———	———	———

9-disc Audio CD Set
This 9-part audio CD set will bring you solutions and to a deeper understanding of the books *Beyond Consequences, Logic, and Control*. These discussions hit the mark for children of all ages and put the concepts of this book into action.
    Price: $97.00

Shipping Costs _____

Total Cost _____

Payable to:

Beyond Consequences Institute
1630A 30th Street, #488
Boulder, CO 80301
www.beyondconsequences.com

Shipping and Handling Scale:
up to $25.00 .... $ 5.95.
$25.01 - $45.00 .... $ 7.95
$45.01 - $90.00 .... $ 9.95
$90.01 - 140.00 .... $ 12.95
$140.01 - 190.00 .... $ 14.95
$190.01 - 240.00 .... $ 16.95
$240.01 - 290.00 .... $ 18.95
over $290.01 .... please call

About the Author
∎

Heather T. Forbes, LCSW

Heather T. Forbes, LCSW, is co-founder and owner of the Beyond Consequences Institute. Forbes has worked with nationally recognized attachment professionals in the field of trauma and attachment since 1999. She is an internationally published author on the topics of adoptive motherhood, raising children with difficult and severe behaviors, and self-development. Forbes lectures, consults, and coaches parents throughout the U.S., Canada, and the U.K., working to create peaceful, loving families. She is passionate about supporting families by bridging the gap between academic research and "when the rubber hits the road" parenting. Much of her experience and insight on understanding trauma, disruptive behaviors, and adoption-related issues comes from her direct mothering experience of her two adopted children.